NONCONFORMITY AND
SOCIAL AND ECONOMIC LIFE
1660—1800

Nonconformity and Social and Economic Life

1660—1800

Some Problems of the Present as they appeared in the Past

By

E. D. BEBB, M.A., Ph.D.

LONDON
THE EPWORTH PRESS
(EDGAR C. BARTON)
25-35 CITY ROAD, E.C.1

First Edition, 1935

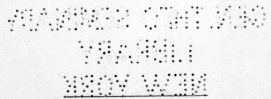

Made and Printed in Great Britain by
Rush & Warwick (Bedford) Ltd., Harpur Printing Works, Bedford.

To
MY FATHER AND MOTHER

SYMBOLS, ABBREVIATIONS and DEFINITIONS

C.H.S.	Congregational Historical Society, *Transactions*.
C.S.P.D.	Calendar of State Papers, Domestic.
D.N.B.	Dictionary of National Biography.
F.H.S.	Friends' Historical Society, *Journal*.
W.H.S.	Wesley Historical Society, *Proceedings*.
BAPTIST MINUTES.	*Minutes of the General Assembly of the General Baptist Church* (edit. W. T. Whitley).
BAXTER : WORKS.	*The Practical Works of the Rev. Richard Baxter* (edit. Wm. Orme).
HIST. MSS. COM.	Historical Manuscripts Commission, *Reports*.
JOURNAL.	*The Journal of the Rev. John Wesley* (edit. Curnock).
LETTERS.	*The Letters of John Wesley* (edit. Telford).
N.H.M.	*A New History of Methodism*, by Townsend, Workman and Eayrs.
PREACHERS.	*The Lives of the Early Methodist Preachers.*
SERMONS.	*The Standard Sermons of John Wesley* (annotated by E. H. Sugden).
WORKS.	*The Works of the Rev. John Wesley* (edit. Thomas Jackson).
DISSENTERS.	This term is used to embrace Presbyterians, Baptists of various sorts, Independents and Congregationalists.
NONCONFORMISTS.	This term is used to include all Denominations of Protestant Nonconformists, Methodists amongst them.

CONTENTS

PREFACE

IT is not true that history repeats itself. Yet the past frequently offers parallels to the present and not least in social and economic matters. Often the latest problems turn out to be those faced by our ancestors in a different context, although they may appear to many to be entirely new owing to their very acuteness. Because human nature varies little, the same problems reappear; because the environment—social, political, economic—is always being modified, so these problems often appear to be more novel than they actually are.

In this period, 1660-1800, a remarkable change took place in the English world. The character of its government altered; the organization of its industry changed; its social structure was varied. During the same period, modern Nonconformity emerged and established itself. The writer does not advance the thesis that these political, economic, and social changes were due to the appearance of Nonconformity. He does, however, seek to show that the part played by Nonconformity was out of all proportion to its size and was of lasting importance. What took place in the consciences of Nonconformists affected contemporary England far more than she realized.

The writer gladly and gratefully acknowledges his indebtedness to Mr. G. P. Jones, M.A., Lecturer in Economic History at Sheffield University, who has offered many invaluable criticisms and suggestions throughout the progress of the book. He is also indebted to the Rev. H. W. Sendall for reading the proofs; to Miss Elsie Potter for help with the Index; and to the Librarian of Dr. Williams's Library, London.

Liphook, Hants.   E. D. BEBB.
March, 1935.

Nonconformity and Social and Economic Life, 1660–1800

CHAPTER I

A CHANGING WORLD

'THE Gospel of Christ knows of no religion but social, no holiness, but social holiness.'[1] A saved soul is a social factor for no man liveth unto himself. That complete change of outlook which is conversion cannot stop short at the person who has experienced it. So religion, one of the most intimate elements in history, when passing through one of its recurrent periods of dynamic activity, often quickens the sense of social and economic responsibility.

The period with which this book deals followed the marked religious excitement and activity of the Puritan Revolution, and, after a few quiet decades, included that new and prolonged outburst of fervour known as the Methodist Revival. This period was also in its earlier phase one of political uncertainty, and in its later was marked by rapid economic change, accentuating social problems. What was the reaction of Nonconformity, the section principally concerned with the religious activity, to these political, economic, and social changes? It is the purpose of this book to investigate this question; a purpose, the achievement of which will show how some of the problems of the present were dealt with in the past.

ECONOMIC AND SOCIAL CHANGES

By the sixteenth century, English goods were being exported almost all over the then-known world. Commercial organization, in regulated and joint-stock companies, was highly developed with a credit and foreign exchange system in

[1] Wesley in his Preface to the Hymn-Book of 1739.

being. Accordingly, the economic life of the country was closely linked with international trade, with the result that already a large proportion of English homes were dependent upon foreign markets for their livelihood.[1] Since the twelfth century the principal English industry had been the woollen, the importance of which could hardly be over-estimated. It provided the means by which this country could participate in foreign trade, and helps to explain the far-reaching agricultural changes of the fifteenth and sixteenth centuries, when the first enclosure movement commenced the alteration of the face of England. In the seventeenth century, the woollen manufacture accounted for over two-thirds of the exports from England, while in the eighteenth, woollen exports grew from about £3,000,000 to about £7,000,000 per annum.[2] So important was the woollen industry that it powerfully affected trade policy, the export of English wool being completely prohibited between 1660 and 1825. This was due to the desire for a plentiful supply of wool at a low price for home manufacture. It was then generally believed that trade depressions resulted, in part at least, from the export of wool, ' whereby the stranger's wheel is set going,' and that if we refused to supply continental countries with the raw material, foreign competition would cease.[3]

The discoveries of silver in America in the mid-sixteenth century led to a serious rise in prices and dislocation of foreign exchanges. It was this rise in prices that underlay the enclosure movement of the period since landed magnates found they could not maintain their standard of living on their former income. The open field system prevented that

[1] Lipson, *The Economic History of England*, II, p. 184.

[2] *ibid*, II, p. 188, ' More precise figures are available for the eighteenth century: they are official values, but serve to show the relative proportions.' They are:—

	General Exports.		Exports of Woollen Goods.
1700	£6,477,402	... ...	£2,989,163
1760	14,694,970	... ...	5,453,172
1800	43,152,019	... ...	6,917,583

[3] *ibid*, III, pp. 28f. The economic policy, if such it may be called, of the sixteenth, seventeenth and eighteenth centuries is known as the ' Mercantile System.' It was a complex of prejudices, propaganda, and partly contradictory opinions, imbued with a strong spirit of nationalism, and affected by the consequences of the silver discoveries in America.

change over to grazing whereby they were able to get a larger return from their land; consequently they sought to enclose the fields. At home, the production of food and raw material, and manufactures, were encouraged by the Corn Laws and by the protection of industry, while the Navigation Acts (especially that of 1651) sought to keep what carrying trade there might be in English bottoms. Under the earlier Stuarts, the regulation of industry was energetically, even if not consistently or effectively, taken in hand. In this there was little new, but a fresh energy was now apparent. The usual way of regulating industry in respect of new discoveries and inventions was by patents of monopoly, while Trading Companies such as the East India Company, the most famous of them all, were formed for the promotion and ordering of foreign trade. By the end of the eighteenth century, Government regulation in industry had diminished.

The eighteenth century witnessed the early phase of the Industrial Revolution. This Revolution both left its mark on Nonconformity and was itself served by it. As the history of the Industrial Revolution has often been written, it is only necessary for our purposes to observe such changes as might raise questions of social responsibility in the minds of Nonconformists. The roots of this Revolution go back much further than 1760, from which time it is conventionally dated. The organization and technique of industry did not suddenly break with previous practice; on the contrary, they formed part of a long process of development.[1] The term 'Revolution' in this connexion is misleading, the evolutionary character of the process being at least as remarkable as its revolutionary aspect. Nor is it correct to assume that the Industrial Revolution was the cause of England's world-wide industrial supremacy for 'long before the Industrial Revolution the reputation of her wares had made England the workshop of the world.'[2] Under the old and gradually superseded system of domestic industry people often worked

---

[1] On large-scale production in the sixteenth and seventeenth centuries, see Nef.: *Economic History Review*, October, 1934. Production had been capitalistically organized and a proletariat was in existence before the coming of the factory system; the old days had gone when every apprentice could look forward to the time when he should be a master.

[2] Lipson, *The Economic History of England*, II, pp. 188f.

appallingly long hours, but they had a valuable sense of freedom and independence. The advent of power-driven machinery, and consequently of factory-life,[1] demanded large aggregations of people removed from their old surroundings. Domestic industry was often worked in conjunction with agriculture, the employment of children being one of its features.

The Industrial Revolution did not bring about child labour, indeed in the long run it had the opposite effect. Under the old system, child labour was considered highly desirable and was widely approved. It was the demand for child labour *in factories* that intensified the hardships of the lives of children and brought into relief their sufferings, as a result of which, step by step, and against great opposition, this form of industrial labour was reduced, controlled, and finally almost abolished. Then under the domestic system, the producer was not so entirely divorced from the means of production as he came to be when wool was no longer spun and woven by the family of the man on the backs of whose sheep it had grown. The old system implied the wide dispersion of industry whereas the new was associated with ever-growing towns, thus giving rise to many social problems. In the Industrial Revolution the expansion of wealth and population was not accompanied by a commensurate rise in the standard of living of those whose labour was employed and sometimes exploited. It was as a consequence of these facts that those movements of thought and feeling which constitute the psychological aspect of the present-day social problem arose.

It is also true that in the earlier period of the Industrial Revolution, men sometimes rose by energy and ability from the position of wage-earners to that of manufacturers, occasionally in a big way. Yet the change over from the one system of production to the other made it increasingly evident that the vast majority could never hope to become masters but must always remain in a subordinate position, both socially and economically. Then in medieval days, production,

---

[1] An Act of 1555 concerning weaving, suggests that something in the nature of a factory system was then growing up—see Bland, Brown and Tawney, *English Economic History, Select Documents,* pp. 320ff.—while individual factories go back much further.

exchange, and distribution had been controlled, often in minute detail if rarely with complete success. It is true that by the time of our period much of this control had ceased, but its tradition was still alive. Now, with the Industrial Revolution, competition was substituted for regulation and one of the old bases of social life was shattered.

One aspect of the Industrial Revolution which has received a great deal of attention concerns inventions, the industry principally affected being cotton.[1] Our interest here, however, in these different technical advances, lies in the changes they brought about in the social environment and in the emergence of social problems with which Nonconformists, like others, would find themselves involved. It was the operatives who were chiefly concerned in that social revolution which was part of the Industrial Revolution. The new machines not only speeded up production and changed its character; they forced the pace of the operatives and changed their outlook. Yet it must be noticed that the new inventions were introduced much more slowly than has often been supposed. This was due not only to a conservative outlook, but also to the imperfection of the new machines and the difficulty of finding sufficient skilled labour to work them. Power-weaving in the woollen manufacture, for instance, did not become a factory industry until the mid-nineteenth century. As the introduction of machinery was so slow it is not surprising to find that it was rarely the sole efficient cause of outbreaks. When these occurred there were usually other grievances present, and the outbreaks tended to be sporadic and discontinuous.

In 1779, there was an attack against Arkwright's invention, and factories were burned in a number of places, so that the military had to be called out. This violence was due, however, not only to the introduction of new machinery, but also to other causes, such as unemployment due to the

[1] Lipson, *The Economic History of England,* II, p. 97 :—' The growth of the cotton industry in the eighteenth century can be measured by the following statistics. The remarkable increase near the end of the century was due to the invention of spinning machinery.'

Cotton Wool Imported.

1701	...	...	...	1,985,868 lbs.
1751	...	...	...	2,976,610
1781	...	...	...	5,198,778
1791	...	...	...	28,706,675
1801	...	...	...	56,004,305

American War. For a time there was some public sympathy with the spinners, and in some places machinery was temporarily discarded. In the south-west, where a fairly prosperous woollen industry was in existence, there was some sporadic destruction of machinery, and wages tended to go down. In Yorkshire, the comparative independence of the spinner prevented a great deal of trouble. It was in the south-eastern counties, Norfolk, Suffolk, and Essex, where most disturbance was experienced, partly due, however, to agrarian causes. On the whole the troubles traceable to the introduction of new spinning machinery and methods were less than might have been expected. In the case of the weavers, disturbances were complicated by wage disputes which had no direct link with the bringing in of machinery. The last major outbursts over the introduction of machinery were the Luddite disturbances, 1811-1813, in a number of different parts of the country. The question arises, did the Nonconformists, as such, modify or affect this social unrest, inevitable when so great an industrial change was in progress? There is, as will be later shown, some evidence that they did.

It is important to remember that England was not urbanized until the nineteenth century, prior to which it was a rural country. The towns of the seventeenth and eighteenth centuries were not only small in size, but were in intimate and conscious relationship with the country around and without that sharp opposition of interest which has often characterized urban and rural life since. The towns were small and industry was largely domestic so that countryman and townsman were alike affected by any change which might occur in conditions. London, it is true, was large in actual size and still larger relatively, its population at the end of the seventeenth century numbering some half million, or a little under one-tenth of the total population of the country. It was not, however, a city of factories, its manufactures being carried on, as else-where, under the domestic system, while its great importance lay in its functions as a port of international trade and a distributing centre for internal trade. In the predominantly rural society of the period there were three main divisions—landlords, yeomanry, and labourers. Of these, the yeomanry at the beginning of our period was very important, whereas by the end had seriously declined. The yeoman was a man whose economic independence had encouraged a sterling independence of character, and who was lavishly praised by his contemporaries. He belonged to a class mid-way between the landed gentry and the labourers, often a freeholder, but sometimes holding his land on lease or copyhold tenure. It is estimated that at the beginning of the eighteenth century there were 170,000 of these cultivators, but by the end of the century nearly all had disappeared. In a great many cases these small farmers had become agricultural labourers, thus descending in both the economic and social scales.

One of the reasons for this remarkable disappearance of the true yeoman of England may have been the Enclosure Movement of the eighteenth, and early nineteenth, centuries. Formerly agricultural improvements had taken a very long time to spread, partly because of the remoteness of many districts and partly because farmers then cultivated much less for markets than now. In many cases markets were far away or otherwise difficult of access, and there was consequently little encouragement to employ better methods whereby to increase production over local requirements. But in the eighteenth century many agricultural improvements were tried and gradually accepted by the farming community. New crops were introduced, stock-breeding became a science, transport improved, enterprise on the part of landlords and farmers increased. At the same time, especially towards the end of the period, population was increasing and the demand for larger supplies of food therefore growing. For agricultural progress, however, one great change in traditional methods was necessary. The ancient system of common field cultivation had to give way to the system of separate occupation—common land had to be enclosed. By these changes rural society was revolutionized. So in order that the increasing manufacturing population might be fed, changes took place which involved the divorce of the peasantry from the soil.

Rural life, and indeed urban life, was also being affected profoundly by the improvement in communications. Social change depends in considerable part upon physical movement. The more rapidly men can get in touch with one another, the more easily does their outlook change, while religious revivals, no less than commerce itself, depend on adequate transport and communications for their rapid spread. It is not without significance that St. Paul, in his missionary journeys, so often went to large commercial and maritime centres. Here, we are concerned only with road and water traffic, since the railways belong to the nineteenth century. For nearly 300 years, the road administration of this country was based mainly on a statute of 1555, which provided that road maintenance should be the responsibility of the parish, the necessary labour to be supplied free by the parishioners, the whole scheme coming under the Justices.

In our period, especially towards the end, the demands on the roads were increasing. This is to be accounted for by the growth of population; improvement in the speed and construction of carriages, making them more common; and the system of stage-coaches which after 1760 became the principal method of getting about. Goods were mostly carried on pack-horses with bales, panniers and the like, slung either side of the animals, which would then move in Indian file, often along causeways of stones, sometimes raised several feet above the road. They went everywhere, horses and asses, often making long journeys such as from Manchester to London, and in parts of the country working to a printed time-table. In addition, multitudes of cattle and sheep passed along these roads, and it is estimated that by the end of the eighteenth century 100,000 cattle and 150,000 sheep annually entered London, with pigs and poultry in vast quantities.

The roads along which all this traffic had to pass were little more than tracks, with many holes, which in wet weather rapidly became bogs, positively dangerous to life and limb, and often almost impassable. It was on such roads as these that John Wesley rode, the greatest traveller in England of his century. Various expedients were tried in order to remedy the situation, but finally a new method of approach was evolved. Instead of roads being the sole concern of the parishes, an Act of 1706 made possible the formation of trusts to take over specified lengths of the roadways, the trusts being empowered to levy tolls. Hence came into being the Turnpike roads, the value of which varied considerably from one trust to another. What was needed as much as anything was an advance in the technique of road-construction and maintenance, and for this the country had to wait until the work of Telford and Macadam in the early days of the nineteenth century.

For centuries there had been a good deal of river and coast-wise traffic, but many of the rivers of Great Britain were difficult for navigation by reason of the hilly nature of the country. Eventually the appearance of England in regard to waterways was changed by the canal construction begun under the Duke of Bridgwater and his engineer Brinley, whose canal system linked together Liverpool, Manchester, Hull, and Bristol, and a great many intervening places. Many other canals were constructed; the Thames and Severn were connected, the Forth and Clyde, while the Caledonian was also made. Over 3,000 miles of canals were constructed in the United Kingdom and Ireland, so that almost every important town was on or near a canal. The economic result was the cheapening of transport charges, so important to the progress of the Industrial Revolution; while social life was affected by the linking up of so many areas and towns.

The major social problem of the eighteenth century was one which persisted throughout its span. The severity of the problem varied as did the common attitude towards it. The Industrial Revolution affected, but did not originate it. That problem was poverty, and it was for the most part regarded as a problem demanding a solution rather than the indication of a human need crying for sympathetic treatment. The needs of the poor have always been regarded as a special concern of the Church, often on theological as well as on philanthropic grounds, for almsgiving might benefit the giver hereafter as well as the recipient now. Our study of social influences of Nonconformity, therefore, has to do with a period when this subject, traditionally the special concern of the Church, was occupying the attention not only of philanthropists but of statesmen, writers, local authorities, and the general public. A national system of poor relief began in the sixteenth century, for by that time the volume of destitution had grown to serious dimensions. The reasons for this are to be found in the widespread change-over from corn-growing to sheep-farming, with its consequent lessened demand for labour; in the increased capitalization of industry and development of foreign trade, combined with a short-sighted Government policy, all resulting in a fluctuating demand for labour; and in changes in the value of money, upsetting the general level of prices. It is not surprising, therefore, that in the sixteenth century beggars went about in swarms, often causing apprehension, to which the nursery rhyme bears witness—

Hark! Hark! the dogs do bark; the beggars are coming to town;
Some gave them white bread, some gave them brown,
And some gave them a good horse-whip, and sent them out of the town.[1]

The 1601 Poor Law Code, which remained the substantial basis of the public treatment of the poor down to the Poor Law Amendment Act, 1834, laid down that the churchwardens, together with two, three, or four substantial householders, were to act as overseers of the poor in each parish, under the authority of the Justices, and were to assess, tax, and have collected a rate from all occupiers of land, houses, and tithes. These officers were to see that the impotent poor were maintained by contributions from the funds while the able-bodied were to be supplied with materials for work, and if the latter would not work they were to be treated as criminals. The overseers were enabled compulsorily to apprentice the children of those who were unable to maintain them. Actually, the work of the parishes for the impotent poor was fairly good, but not for the unemployed able-bodied, a state of affairs to be expected since a parish would be too small a unit for the purpose.

Owing to causes, as yet not exhaustively examined, effective central control tended to disappear during the seventeenth century. One difficulty which arose in administration resulted from the migration of poor people, looking for work or in search of a wealthier or more generous parish. An attempt to solve this difficulty was made in 1662 by the Act of Settlement. According to this, local Justices, on the complaint of the overseers, might with certain exceptions return any poor person coming into a given parish, within forty days, to the parish in which such person had a settlement by birth, apprenticeship, or domestic service. This tended to tie a man down to his own locality and was designed to prevent persons

[1] Lipson, op. cit., III, p. 422, quoted from Ashley, An Introduction to English Economic History and Theory (1909), II, p. 352.

easily obtaining a settlement in different places, and in its
operation was a continual source of contention between neigh-
bouring parishes. What was needed was a larger unit for
relief, a group of parishes instead of so many acting
separately. In 1722, an Act was passed which provided a
workhouse test. Any parish might set up a workhouse and
any poor person refusing to live in it and work there ceased
to have a claim on relief.

Sixty years later Gilbert's Act made the treatment milder
and distinguished between different classes of the poor.
Under it suitable treatment was to be provided for the old,
infirm, and for children, in institutions for which parishes
might join together. The able-bodied were to be found work,
and if they refused were to be sent to the House of Correction.
The responsibility for the poor was vested in certain elected
gentlemen who were to supervise the overseers. Thus began
to go the isolation of the single parish, while the domination,
sometimes very harsh, of the parish officer, was restricted. A
new source of administrative chaos was the benevolent action,
much condemned by Poor Law reformers, of the Berkshire
Justices in 1795. Meeting at Speenhamland, they declined to
regulate labourers' wages, as they were empowered to do by
an old Statute, but resolved instead to grant relief, where
necessary, on a scale based on the price of bread.[1] This action
of the Berkshire Justices was so widely copied that it was
more effective than some of the Acts of Parliament passed in
respect of poor relief. Not until 1834 were radical changes
made in the legal attitude towards the poor and the manner
and scale of their relief. The history of Nonconformity in
the later part of the seventeenth and in the eighteenth
centuries brought it into special relation to poverty, and we
shall see the ways in which it responded.

POLITICAL CHANGES

The sixteenth century saw the establishment by the Tudors
of a strong monarchy, supreme over the nobility, master of
the Church, and acknowledged as the sole and sufficient
defender of the realm to which it brought, on the whole,

[1] *The Reading Mercury*, May 11, 1795. Also quoted in Brown, Bland
and Tawney, *op. cit.*, pp. 655f.

freedom from civil strife. The accession of James I began a long constitutional struggle; this was followed by a series of constitutional experiments immediately preceding our particular period. James, and his son Charles, held the theory of the Divine Right of Kings which did not agree well with either English history or the English temper. The Tudors had asserted an absolute monarchy it is true, but their assertion was tempered by political sagacity, while the Spanish threat, until the Armada had been defeated, made people more ready to acquiesce in their claim.

Now James and Charles claimed a complete freedom of control from law. Personal royal responsibility became political irresponsibility. This aggression on the part of the Crown stimulated the aggressiveness of Parliament, and a contest was sooner or later unavoidable. Moreover, the growing Puritanism was opposed to such a royal conception, because of the innate respect for law which Puritanism had, for rigid rules, and for the personal responsibility of the individual—which implied his freedom. To the Puritan, the theory of divine right was politically indefensible, morally wrong, and essentially irreligious. Parliamentary opposition led both James and Charles to govern for long periods without summoning Parliament, a policy that was possible as long as the monarch could manage on the traditional sources of Royal income, or could be exactions and expedients supplement it sufficiently. When more revenue than this brought in was required, however, Parliament had to be summoned.

Crown and Parliament clashed over both money and religion, and this connexion between money and religion was not adventitious. The Puritans, as we shall see, felt the practice of their religion to be particularly concerned with the right and responsible use of wealth. In their view wealth might not be used as a means to selfish, and often voluptuous gratification, as it sometimes was by Stuart kings. James, while on the Scottish throne before the Union of 1603, had been so often rebuked and frustrated by the Presbyterians of the Northern Kingdom that he was predisposed to resent and to fight any who were not content with the *status quo* of the Anglican Church. Charles, who was ready to favour the Catholics, and who married a Catholic princess, further estranged himself from his Puritan subjects. Religion, money, and politics, were at the time interwoven in a very intimate way. In regard to each of these, save for a brief spell at Charles' accession, opposition grew between the two successive monarchs and a large part of the nation. Whereas Charles I was less Protestant than his father, England had become more so, although the Laudian policy of persecution harried the Puritans sorely.

After eleven years of personal rule, Charles was forced, in 1640, to summon Parliament because of rebellion in Scotland, shortness of money, and widespread unrest in England. This, the Long Parliament, set to work to undo Charles' policy, to re-assert the fundamental liberties of the people and to win for itself new powers. The result was Civil War. With the fortunes of this war we are not concerned. What is important to an understanding of the position of the Dissenters later, is to note the league with Scotland, whereby the Parliamentary side secured the aid of a Scotch army. To win this, consent had to be given to the adoption in England of the Presbyterian system of Church government which the Commons did by accepting the Solemn League and Covenant. Such an agreement was necessary between these two nations, but it raised problems giving rise soon to much bitterness and strife.

Later, when Cromwell had the government in his hands, he showed that he wanted both liberty of conscience and an established Church, and on the whole was surprisingly successful in achieving this end. The Presbyterian system had, in fact, failed to take over on the downfall of Episcopacy, and Cromwell set up a Board of Triers, to examine the fitness of candidates for livings. Under this body, both Presbyterian and Independent ministers were presented to livings, while even Quakers found the Protector sympathetic to them. We need not be detained by the various methods by which Cromwell attempted to organize the government of the country. They rapidly succeeded one another, and ceased with his death. Oliver dead, the short fiasco of Richard over, Monk restored Charles II to the throne.

The return of Charles II was popular, many people being tired of the Puritan regime. None the less they did not want to revert to pre-Commonwealth conditions, nor did such conditions in fact return. The Prerogative Courts of Star Chamber and High Commission were not revived, while taxation could no longer be imposed without consent of Parliament. The balance of power between King and Parliament was more even than formerly, but it was an uneasy balance. Parliament had the purse and could legislate, but the executive was in royal hands, and State action largely depended upon the monarch's will, especially in regard to wars and foreign affairs generally. During this reign the fear of insurrection was not infrequent, and actual outbreaks did occur. After a short rule, James II, who lacked the political sense of his brother, left the Kingdom, never to return, in December, 1688. To the turbulence of the times, natural enough in a century that was witnessing such drastic political changes, were added years of repression and persecution of the Nonconformists, under the series of Acts known as the Clarendon Code. What result did it produce on them? How far was their loyalty strained? Many regarded them as political traitors as well as religious nuisances, and this is a charge which we shall investigate.

The Revolution Settlement of 1689, when William and Mary ascended the throne, proved to be a lasting one. With it the long strife between Crown and Parliament diminished so that although friction remained, the two became partners in government, with Parliament predominant. The Settlement was characterized by moderation, of which the Toleration Act of that year was an outstanding example, under which freedom of worship, with some limitations, was granted. Law, not arbitrary power, was now coming into its supremacy. With the detailed political changes, and the struggles of Tory and Whig in Anne's reign, we are not here concerned. The intolerance of the powerful Tory party in the last years of that reign bade fair to produce another period of religious persecution, but the Queen's death and the accession of George I altered that. The Hanoverians were strongly supported by the Whigs who now had half a century of power in front of them with the Dissenters as allies.

Until the failure of the 1745 Stuart invasion, the Hanoverian tenure of the throne was never quite certain, a state of affairs which, as we shall see, had repercussions on the

Dissenters. Thereafter, for the rest of the century, political movements in this country did not seriously affect the social attitude and influence of the Nonconformist bodies. The 1689 Settlement had important social influences as well as political consequences. The illegalities of James II in respect of the Church, the municipalities, the Universities, and property, evoked by reaction a powerful regard for law, for vested interests, and anything settled and stable which seemed likely to provide a bulwark against any subsequent attempt on the part of the prerogative to over-ride the law. Fixed standards, tending to become sacrosanct; stability, resulting in some stagnation, were the consequences.

James II had tried to bend the local gentry, the squires, to his will, especially in the matter of the furtherance of Roman Catholicism, and the Revolution of 1688 was the answer, following which throughout the whole of our period and beyond, there was little attempt on the part of the central executive to direct or control the local administration of the squires acting in the capacity of Justices of the Peace. These squires, Tory for the most part, were appointed by the Crown acting through the Lord Chancellor—Hanoverian appointments through a Whig oligarchy—the central authorities being sensible enough not to attempt to repeat the mistake of the last Stuart king. Had these Justices been paid officials, the situation might have been different, but while they were given their appointment by Whitehall, they had to maintain themselves. This meant that rural England was under aristocratic rule. Political and social power in eighteenth-century England was thus concentrated into the hands of one class largely, the landowners. Yet there was no class hatred, partly because of the many different social levels which existed between the highest and lowest, and partly because the class barriers, although real, were not rigid. The Industrial Revolution changed the predominantly rural nature of English society into one chiefly industrial and urban. This tended towards democratic development since the eighteenth-century aristocracy, based on land ownership, had no special advantages in the new order of things.[1]

[1] Trevelyan, *History of England*, p. 514.

Ecclesiastical Changes

Contemporaneous with the above there were ecclesiastical changes. Tudor policy might aim at comprehensiveness, but it could not provide a spiritual home for all types of religious outlook and experience. Many sects appeared, in some cases distinguished only by slight differences, and the life of many of them was obscure and short. There emerged, however, in the sixteenth and seventeenth centuries four bodies destined to play an important part in the internal life of the country, and to this number the eighteenth century added a fifth. These were the Presbyterians, Independents, Baptists, Quakers, and Methodists. Of these, the Presbyterians alone aimed at a change in national Church government, seeking to substitute the Presbyteral for the Episcopal method.

The acceptance by the House of Commons in 1643 of the Presbyterian form of Church government implied a change in administration and not an abrogation of the Church of England. The Presbyterians desired no toleration of Dissenters; in fact they loved the Independents as little as they did the Episcopalians. If they regarded the latter as unscriptural, they regarded the former as anarchical. Most people then felt that to be a dissident in religion was a spiritual mistake and a political danger. A sectary was regarded as a potential public enemy. So even while the Civil War was in progress, Parliament pressed on with the new system of ecclesiastical government and the Westminster Assembly of 1643-48 was summoned. The Assembly's recommendations, closely similar to the organization, discipline and doctrine of the Scotch Church, were accepted by Parliament. Nevertheless, the Presbyterian system in spite of Parliamentary effort did not capture the country, and it was only in London and Lancashire that we find it functioning in anything like its complete form. Nor did many years elapse before Presbyterians themselves were classified as Dissenters.

The mid-seventeenth century saw a sudden and powerful expansion of the Independents and Baptists, and many of these men were amongst the best soldiers of the Parliamentary army and hence important both from the military and political points of view. They could no more be made to conform to a national Presbyterian than to a national Episcopal Church.

The terms ' Congregational ' and ' Independent ' came into common use at about the commencement of the Civil War, and these terms are usually employed almost interchangeably. These Independents were advanced Puritans who separated themselves from the Church of England in the latter half of the sixteenth century under such men as Robert Browne, John Greenwood, Henry Barrowe, and Wm. Brewster. The principal mark of Independency was its church polity rather than its belief, although the former was the outcome of the latter. Believing in the complete sufficiency of the Bible as the rule of faith and conduct, it was deduced that the same source would provide all that it was necessary to know concerning Church organization. The conclusion was reached that Scripture knew nothing of a National Church, but only of local associations of Christian men and women, having Christ as their direct Head. Therefore, each local congregation was a true autonomous Church. Under the Cromwellian regime of comparative religious toleration, Independency had its chance and flourished.

Amongst those who were of the Independent way of thinking appeared the Baptists, whose special position rested upon the contention that no one can become a Christian without a conscious act of his own will—hence the opposition to infant baptism. This amounts to a claim for the entire responsibility of each individual before God, and to them belongs the honour of the first assertion in English of the full principle of the liberty of the individual conscience. The General, or Arminian, Baptists began in Amsterdam in 1611 by a split from the Independents there, while the Particular, or Calvinistic, Baptists similarly began in London about 1638. On the Continent, the Anabaptist movement, which was strongly socialistic, was distinct from the Baptist, but in England the terms were not usually sharply differentiated. Baptist and Independent are distinguished not only by the insistence of the former upon adult baptism, but also by the Baptist strong connexional sense, with the exercise of authority by a central Assembly representing the whole.

Of the principal sects, the most hated and most persecuted was the Quaker. This body arose out of the life and teaching of George Fox, who began his itinerant ministry in 1647, and who would have none of parish priest or State Church, be it episcopal or presbyterian. The Quaker religion was mystical but eminently practical. Believing in the reality and imperative nature of a directing Inner Light and in a life in accord with their interpretation of the Bible, Quakers were citizens of the most obstinate character. Their manner and words were often extravagant, even in an age of theological exuberance, while their refusal to bear arms or to take oaths rendered them politically suspect. Small in numbers, until towards the end of the seventeenth century, they survived all opposition and persecution by their power of enduring affliction and the intransigence of their opinions and conduct. In the eighteenth century we find them equally keen in business and philanthropy, but shorn of their extravagance even while retaining some of their distinctive customs and habits.

The passing of the Act of Uniformity in 1662 placed all four bodies in the same category of being Nonconformists as regards the Church of England. The Methodists must be regarded also as Nonconformists although John Wesley himself lived and died within the Anglican fold, and wished his Societies to remain there too. But almost from the beginning of Methodism, in 1738, its inevitable Nonconformity became annually more certain. The facts of its history were too strong, so that while Wesley clung to his Mother Church he was forced to act in such a way as made allegiance to her on the part of his followers ultimately impossible. Moreover, Methodism was a form of Puritanism from which the Anglican Church of the eighteenth century was constantly moving away, although some of its members retained the temper of, and to some degree modelled their conduct upon, Puritanism. In Methodism we find the perennial desire for a God-filled and God-directed life bursting out after the arid years of the second and third decades of the eighteenth century.

The 140 years from 1660-1800 are of great significance for modern social history because during this time were laid the foundations on which have since developed the social institutions and outlook of our day. Constitutional government drove the old monarchical absolutism from the field. The agricultural face of England was in some areas changed by the enclosure of the open fields. The domestic system of industry received its death blow and the factory had come to stay. During this period, education ceased to be the exclusive responsibility and prerogative of the State Church, and technical and commercial education began. The ancient prison system, or rather lack of system, was shaken. Inroads had been made on the venerable organization of parish poor relief, and a new method and conception of poor relief was about to be enacted. Before the eighteenth century closed, slavery, though not yet abolished, was doomed, and smuggling checked.

During these same 140 years, Nonconformity as a social force developed its modern characteristics. Prior to 1660, it was associated rather with political and ecclesiastical changes than with social and economic development, but the persecutions which followed the Restoration destroyed Nonconformity's political power, except as expressed by its votes at elections. During the eighteenth century, Nonconformity became more and more entrenched among the poorer classes. It is true that not a few of its adherents were amongst those who rose from obscurity to affluence in the earlier phase of the Industrial Revolution. One might expect, therefore, to find that the Nonconformity of the period was of some importance, not only for contemporary life, but also as a factor in the development of twentieth-century social England. The following chapters endeavour to show how far this expectation is justified.

Chapter II

THE NUMBERS OF NONCONFORMISTS: 1660-1800

Any estimate of the influence exerted by religious bodies upon social conditions must take into account a variety of factors, some personal and some material. The personalities of founders, such as St. Francis of Assisi, Calvin and Fox, and of local or subordinate leaders, such as the Independent ministers in the seventeenth century and some of Wesley's preachers in the eighteenth, are clearly important. So also may be the social and economic status and the political power both of leaders and rank and file, as well as their knowledge of affairs and capacity for organizing. Another main cause of the effectiveness of a religious body is likely to be the degree of discipline and unity it possesses, as both Jesuit and Methodist history suggests. Differences of creed also affect the degree and direction of social influence. Another factor of importance is numerical strength. It is no doubt true that a large Laodicean Church may exercise less influence than a small but fervent body, yet even so the range and depth of influence of both is likely to be related to their numbers. The greater the number of those whose beliefs are similar, the more is it probable that they will create a common tradition and strengthen existing customs, even in cases where positively they may contribute little, and with this any social innovator must reckon.

In this period it is difficult to obtain satisfactory data for statistical inquiry, contemporary estimates being rarely the result of exact computation. The persecutions of the latter part of the seventeenth century made it unlikely that accurate figures could easily be obtained, since the difficulties of the times would encourage Dissenters to be reticent. The eighteenth century was a period of wide difference of opinion on population in general, although we may expect the Nonconformist bodies to have had some definite idea as to whether their Churches were growing or declining. This numerical estimate of Nonconformity may be conveniently studied in three periods, the critical time from 1660 to the end of the century; from 1700 to 1740, the period between the life-and-death struggle of Dissent and the rise of Methodism; and from 1740 to the end of the eighteenth century, approximately the period of Wesley's evangelical career.

First Period : 1660-1700

At the Restoration, Dissent was strong in London. In the country its strength was considerable, although varying, sometimes remarkably, between one area and another. The first available figures, after 1660, have to do with the ejectment of ministers, culminating in 1662. It is still uncertain exactly how many lost their livings then, but probably a little over 2,000.[1] The relative magnitude of this number must be taken as an index of the widespread character of those beliefs and opinions which prevented conformity to the Established Church. From this figure, however, little can be deduced as to the number of Dissenters in the country at the time, since the following of these men had varied enormously, nor did they all become ministers of Dissenting congregations.

In 1672, Charles II issued a Declaration of Indulgence under which Dissenting ministers, and places for Dissenting worship, might be licensed. It should be noted that Quakers did not take out licences. Before the Declaration they had held their meetings publicly for the most part, content to suffer if need be,[2] and after the Declaration they simply continued the same practice. Then there may have been other Nonconformists who did not take out licences, while licences were occasionally refused, chiefly in the case of notoriously disaffected fanatics. Further, there are inaccuracies in the records owing to duplication. While, therefore, a perfectly accurate list of those who obtained licences at this time cannot be obtained, a suggestive picture of the state of Nonconformity in 1672 is presented. Careful estimates indicate that the

[1] Bate : *The Declaration of Indulgence.* Appendix 2 and Introduction (by C. H. Firth) p. 9. Matthews, A. G. : *Calamy Revised,* Introduction, pp. 12f.
[2] Society of Friends : *Extracts from the Book of Christian Discipline,* pp. 32, 34.

south-eastern and south-western corners of England were strong for Dissent, but that the northern counties and Wales were weak. The Presbyterians appear as strong around London, in the West Country, in Lancashire and Yorkshire, but weak along the East Coast from the Scottish border as far south as Suffolk, with the exception of Yorkshire. Congregationalists and Independents were strong in Norfolk, Suffolk, Gloucestershire, Bedfordshire, and in London. Comparatively speaking they were also strong in Wales, where about two-thirds of the licences issued were given to them. The Baptists were to be found chiefly in Kent, Somersetshire, Lincolnshire, Wiltshire, and Norfolk.[1]

The Minutes of the General Assembly of the General Baptist Churches in England enable us to get a picture of the size and distribution of that small but not unimportant body, shortly after the Declaration of Indulgence.[2]

The stronghold of this section of Baptists was in Kent, where they had forty-four churches. Of these, twenty-six report their membership totalling 3,513 persons, an average of 135 per church. It was in Kent, too, that the denomination had its largest reported church, at Chatham, which claimed 444 members.[3] Other counties in which the General Baptists

---

[1] Bate: *op. cit.* (Appendix 7). This writer's investigations may be summarized as follows:—

LICENCES ISSUED TO INDIVIDUALS.

		Presby- terian.	Congre- gational.	Indepen- dent.	Bap- tist.	Ana- bapt.	Total
England	...	872	324	50	96	107	1,457 a
Wales	...	9	24	9	2	4	48
Total	...	884 b	348	59	98	111	1,508 a b

a. includes 8 not named.   b. includes 3 Channel Islands.

LICENCES ISSUED IN RESPECT OF PLACES.

England	...	861	219	49	35	34	1,269 c
Wales	...	8	26	3	—	3	41 d
Total	...	869	245	52	35	37	1,310 c d

c. includes 71 not named.   d. includes 1 not named.

See also Matthews, A. G.: *op. cit.,* Introduction, p. 15.

[2] *Baptist Minutes,* see Vol. I, intro., pp. 56-67.

[3] The Baptist figures for Kent show discrepancies. In 1672, twenty-six Baptist churches and ministers obtain licences, while a year or so later there are forty-four General Baptist churches alone, and in 1715 there are eighteen or twenty-seven, according to different reckonings (see Appendix II). Perhaps many of these General Baptist churches were very small and probably were only just coming into existence post-1672 and may either have ceased to exist, or have been overlooked, in 1715.

were relatively strong were Buckinghamshire with twenty-eight churches, Leicestershire with thirty-two, Lincolnshire with thirty-three, and Sussex with eighteen. The whole denomination reported 229 churches, and of this number 106 gave their membership amounting to 7,128, an average of sixty-nine. These returns indicate the way in which the smaller denominations of the period could be spread over different parts of the country, leaving whole counties, and groups of counties, untouched. These General Baptists had not reached the North, and were very few in the West or in East Anglia. Their returns also show the smallness of the average congregation of Baptists, while we have reason to believe that other denominations tended to a higher average.[1]

In 1689 a return was made by the Bishops to King William III of the number of Conformists, Nonconformists and Papists, respectively, in the two Provinces.[2] Sir Peter Pett, a friend of Sir. Wm. Petty, discussing these figures for Canterbury, says the aim was to ascertain the number of heads of families, or housekeepers, so that while a man and his wife might be included, none under the age of sixteen, nor many sons or daughters, lodgers or servants were returned.[3] According to these figures the Protestant Nonconformists were in the proportion of 1 to 22.8 of the Conformists, or 4.386 per cent.[4] As the percentage of Nonconformists to Conformists in the two Provinces is exactly the same, and as no figures by Dioceses are given for the Northern Province, it seems certain that the figure given for York is purely artificial. The percentage of Papists to Conformists, .56, will similarly be found to be identical in each Province. As anything in the nature of a religious census was likely to give rise to

---

[1] See *infra*, p. 38.

[2] *C.S.P.D.*, 1693, pp. 448-450 (State Papers Domestic, King William's Chest 14, No. 89). The figures are :—

Province.	Conformists.	Non-conformists.	Papists.
Canterbury	... 2,123,362	93,151	11,878
York	353,892	15,525	1,978
	2,477,254	108,676	13,856

[3] Petty: *Several Essays in Political Arithmetic* (see *The Economic Writings of Sir William Petty*, edited by C. H. Hull, II, p. 461).

[4] Some discussion of these figures may be found in Lecky: *History of England in the Eighteenth Century*, I, p. 202.

evasion, through the fear of persecution, it seems likely that the figures for Nonconformists (i.e. in the Province of Canterbury, for which genuine returns appear to have been made) should be greater than in this return. The figures for the several dioceses show the percentage of Nonconformists to Conformists to fall within the following limits, viz.,

Over 10 p.c.   Canterbury.
7½ p.c.—10 p.c.   London.
5 p.c.—7½ p.c.   Winchester, Rochester.
2½ p.c.— 5 p.c.   Norwich, Lincoln, Ely, Chichester, Salisbury, Exeter, Bath and Wells, Worcester, Coventry and Lichfield, Gloucester, Bristol, Oxford, St. David's.
Under 2½ p.c.   Hereford, Peterborough, Llandaff, Bangor, St. Asaph.

A comparison of these percentages with the number of Licences issued in 1672 confirms the view that Dissent was relatively strong in London and in the south-east of England, and that it was decidedly weak in Wales. On the other hand, they do not agree in regard to the West of England, where Dissent was almost certainly much stronger than the Bishops' Survey would suggest.

From the Declaration of Indulgence to the end of the century there was a rapid growth of Dissent, one of its features being the luxuriant development of new, or fanatical sects. The greater liberty towards the close of the seventeenth century naturally provided opportunity for the vitality in Dissent, which persecution had failed to stamp out, to find ample scope, not always along conventional lines.

No statistics of Quakers were kept. It is estimated that about the year 1660 there were some 6,000 to 8,000 adult male Quakers, with a total Quaker population of all ages of 30,000 to 40,000.[1] The writer responsible for this estimate considers that their total number had increased by some 10,000 by 1670-1679, but he does not believe any further increase took place after the Toleration Act, a state of things partly to be accounted for by the large and continuous emigration to America.[2] Another estimate arrives at the figure of 100,000 as the total of Quakers in 1700 in the three

[1] Braithwaite: *The Beginnings of Quakerism*, p. 512.
[2] Braithwaite: *The Second Period of Quakerism*, p. 459.

Kingdoms.[1] It is certain that a considerable decline took place in their ranks in the eighteenth century.

We find, then, that during the last forty years of the seventeenth century Dissent was growing, especially in the years immediately following the Act of Toleration of 1689.[2] It was strongest in the more populous and wealthier districts, and was notably weak in the North except for the Presbyterian interest in Lancashire and Yorkshire. Between 1673 and 1700, the total number of Dissenters may with confidence be put at over 150,000, with a maximum probably of 250,000. The lower figure would give an average congregation of 115 for each of the places licensed in 1672, while some of the Dissenting congregations are known to have been large, and in 1715 their average seems to have approached 300.[3] In addition there were the Quakers.

SECOND PERIOD : 1700-1740

In the early eighteenth century Nonconformity was ebbing. In spite of the persecutions they had endured and the liberty for which they stood, in many respects the Dissenters were quite conservative. Their theology had varied little while their public worship tended to lose a good deal of fervour as the dangers attending it disappeared. Then the first two decades of the eighteenth century saw the disaffection of many Dissenting ministers. Freedom of inquiry was now more possible, and it produced not only differences of opinion but sometimes virulent dissension. A MS. of 1731, by a London writer, says that a number of ministers 'admit all sorts of persons that will but say they are Christians into their communion, be they Arminians, Calvinists, Freethinkers, Arians, or Socinians, it is all one to them, and their pulpits too are ready to receive ministers of the same make.' The same writer asserts that there were at that time in London forty-four Presbyterian ministers, of whom nineteen were Calvinist, thirteen Arminian, and twelve held a mixture of both views. He says, however, that nearly all the thirty-three London Independent ministers were Calvinist.[4] Some of the

---

[1] Turner : *The Quakers*, p. 244.   [2] See Appendix I.   [3] See *infra*, p. 38.
[4] Anon : *A View of the Dissenting Interest in London*, pp. 87-92. For a description of this MS. see *infra*, pp. 39f.

younger ministers began to conform, and in consequence it not infrequently happened that the congregations of which they had been the pastors ceased to exist. Butler and Secker were among those who turned to the Established Church about this time, while Arianism had probably become fairly widespread amongst the ministers. A significant and marked change appeared amongst the Presbyterians in the early years of the eighteenth century, when a large part of that denomination was extinguished, following the Salter Hall Conference of 1719.[1] Unitarianism then got such a hold in the churches that the Unitarians were able to become organized as a distinct body of churches in England.[2] Decline had also set in among the Quakers so that one of their leaders wrote in 1723, ' Whereas it hath been observed that our week-day meetings are thinner now than they were thirty or forty years ago . . . the present age produceth another sort of men, who have little regard to religion.'[3] As is not infrequent in times of religious decline, the contraction was hardly noticeable for some while, and the effects of the numerical and spiritual shrinkage of 1700-1740 became more apparent after the latter date.

For this and the next period it is possible to obtain, not accurate statistics, but a sufficiently reliable estimate to present an intelligible picture of the numerical relation of the Nonconformists to the nation at large. Fortunately there exists in manuscript form the whole, or part, of three contemporary estimates of the state of Dissent, covering the years 1715-16 and 1772-73. In these MSS. returns appear not only from each county, but from more than one corres-

---

[1] This Conference was held on February 19, 1719, in the Salters' Hall, London, and was attended by over 150 ministers. The occasion was an inquiry into the heterodoxy of a Presbyterian minister, one James Peirce of Exeter, whose anti-Trinitarian views had become known. Exeter laid the matter before the London Dissenting ministers. The Conference split in two, and from that time Arianism, developing into Unitarianism, advanced with remarkable rapidity. No attempt had been made after the Revolution to revive the Presbyterian Church organization and government which left individual Presbyterian churches much less able to withstand the move towards Arianism—see Drysdale : *The Presbyterians in England*, p. 198.

[2] Independents and Baptists, as well as Presbyterians, became Unitarians.

[3] Bellers : *Epistle to the Yearly, Quarterly, and Monthly Meetings of Great Britain*, p. 1.

pondent in the case of some counties. Sometimes the figures
supplied by these different correspondents are almost
identical or in substantial agreement, while at other times there
is considerable divergence. Where this divergence exists it
may be due to the relative remoteness of some districts, one
correspondent being very familiar with one part of a scattered
area, whereas another would know more about a different
part. Where two sets of figures exist for the same county,
unless there is evidence that the higher is more reliable, the
lower has been taken for the purpose of this inquiry, since
in the absence of scientifically compiled statistics an over-
estimate seems more probable than an under-estimate. It
seems probable that we may rely on the general accuracy of
these lists.[1] Unfortunately, all the correspondents do not give
full information. In the case of some counties in the Evans
List (1715-16) no figures are given of the size of congregations ('hearers') or only of a few. Similarly in respect of
the social, economic, and political importance of adherents.
Sufficient is given, however, to enable the reader to obtain a
fair idea of the actual state of the Dissenting interest at those

[1] They are the 'Records of Nonconformity,' in Dr. Williams's Library,
London, numbered respectively 4, 5, and 6. No. 4 gives the returns
obtained from an inquiry instituted in 1715 by the Dissenters themselves
of which the centre was naturally in London. The method adopted was
to have correspondents in each county who made returns to the compiler
in London, a Dr. John Evans. Evans was colleague, and then successor
to Dr. Daniel Williams of the important Hand Alley Presbyterian church.
Most of those correspondents whose names appear in the MS. seem to
have been Paedobaptists, which may account for the fact that the
information concerning the Baptists is meagre compared with that given
in respect of the Presbyterian and Independent bodies. A mass of
information is also given respecting the social composition of the
Dissenters of the time, their wealth in many cases, and very often their
voting strength. No. 5 contains a comparative statement for the years
1715 and 1773, when another such 'census' was taken. Appendices II and
III give in addition to the Evans figures, those of another compilation of
the same period (i.e. 1715) made by Daniel Neal, author of the *History
of the Puritans,* whose original MS. is not known to be in existence, but
whose figures are preserved in this MS. by the Rev. Josiah Thompson
(on whom see *infra* p. 40), the man responsible both for this book and
the next, No. 6, which gives the 1773 estimate, and therefore covers to
some extent the same ground as No. 5.
    The scarcity of other statistical material makes it impossible to state
the value of these three records very exactly. The compilers evidently
took great pains to get trustworthy figures. Those independently arrived
at by Evans and Neal, although differing in the case of a number of
counties, in the aggregate agree fairly closely, while the Thompson List
gives a mass of descriptive detail which both illustrates and confirms the
numerical results.

periods. Owing to the alternative figures given for some counties, the erasures and alteration of some of the figures, and the illegibility of others, it is possible to arrive at different totals from an examination of the MSS., and those writers who have dealt with them have usually reached slightly varying results.[1] Nevertheless, the possible different readings are not such as to prevent a reasonably accurate result being obtained. Unfortunately the number of 'hearers,' the term used by the correspondents, is not given for all congregations, but it is perhaps a fair assumption that those congregations for which no figures are given are likely to have been small. The county correspondents would probably have information of the larger and more accessible congregations. The Thompson List (1773) gives less statistical but more descriptive information.

The number of congregations in 1715 in England and Wales for which figures are given in the Evans List is about 780, amounting to nearly 230,000 hearers, an average per congregation of a little more than 290.[2] In the Neal List there are 1,089 separate congregations while Evans gives some 1,100 pastoral charges. If the unreported congregations were as a rule smaller than the reported, the total number of hearers amongst the Dissenters in 1715 may have been rather less than 300,000.[3] In Wales, as in the case of England, it seems possible that unreported congregations are likely to have been small. On the other hand, the remoteness of some districts may have meant that a fairly large church could have existed without the correspondent being aware of more than

[1] Most writers who have dealt with these MSS. have been concerned with special points of view, and therefore have made use of part of the material only. Amongst these are Fryer: *The Numerical Decline of Dissent in England;* Rees: *History of Protestant Nonconformity in Wales; Transactions of the Baptist Historical Society,* Vol. II, No. 2, 95ff, and Vol. VI, No. 2, 161; and *Congregational Historical Society,* V, pp. 206 and 385.

[2] See Appendices II, III.

[3] We know from these MSS. that some congregations were large. A considerable number were over 750 and several were over 1,000, viz.: Bedford (Ind.) 1,200; Cambridge (Ind.) 1,100; Chester 1,000; Dean Row, near Stockport, 1,309; Manchester 1,550; Liverpool 1,158; Bolton 1,094; Chowbent, Atherton, 1,064; Hand Alley, London, 1,000; Nottingham 1,400; Bristol 1,600 and 1,200 (Anabp.); Taunton 2,000; Frome 1,000; Gosport (Ind.) 1,000; Sheffield 1,163; Neath (Ind.) 1,006. Unless otherwise stated these were Presbyterian churches.

its name.[1] It is difficult to decide what value should be given to the term 'hearers.' In a few cases in the MS. the composition of the hearers is stated as so many men, so many women, and so many children, apparently the term including children as well as adults. Sufficient cases are not, however, given to make this sure, and the practice of different county correspondents may have varied. We ought probably to take the number of hearers as estimated from the MS. as representing the number of those who were zealous Dissenters, realizing that there would be others who came within the ambit of Dissent. It must be remembered in regard to the above figures that they include neither the Quakers nor the lesser sects.

Under the Toleration Act all new places of worship established by the Dissenters had to be registered. From the returns,[2] it would appear that in this Second Period, 1700-1740, the old Dissent had reached its zenith, probably in the early years of the eighteenth century in the first decade of which 1,219 temporary and forty-one permanent places of their worship were registered in England and Wales, figures which had shrunk to 424 and twenty-four, respectively, for the decade 1731-1740. It was not until the Evangelical Revival had got into its stride that renewed growth was manifested, though that growth was not necessarily due to the Revival.

Conditions in London are to some extent revealed by a MS. of 1731, compiled by an unknown Dissenter who in 105 pages compares the state of Dissent in the capital in the years 1695 and 1731.[3] The chief reason for this work is stated by the writer to have been the 'prevailing humour of some people which they were officiously spreading (viz.) That this Interest is in a very low and declining condition . . . particularly as to the number of persons that attend on public worship on the Lord's day.' He describes each Dissenting chapel in turn, giving details concerning the buildings,

[1] *The Cambridge Modern History,* VI, p. 81. A notable revival began in Wales about the year 1735, due largely to Griffith Jones. The Neal List for Wales gives forty-three congregations (or pastorates) but this appears to be incomplete.

[2] Appendix I.

[3] MS., Anon: *A View of the Dissenting Interest in London,* pp. 79f (Dr. Williams's Library, 'Records of Nonconformity,' No. 18).

pastors, and congregations. He summarizes his conclusions as follows :

Congregations	increased since 1695	...	...	...	13
do.	declined since 1695	...	...	...	15
do.	varied little since 1695	...	...	...	18
do.	ceased since 1695	...	...	...	11
do.	new since 1695	...	...	...	10
Meeting-houses	in 1695	...	...	...	57
do.	in 1731	...	...	...	58

He estimates that in this period the seating accommodation had increased by some 4,000, but admits that the population of London in the same period had increased proportionally much more. Concerning the Baptists, the writer states they had twenty-five meeting-houses of which two observed the seventh day as the Sabbath. Of the twenty-three remaining, eight were General and fifteen Particular Baptists. 'Their congregations are considerably smaller than either the Presbyterians or the Independents, and the people are generally of lower stations in life.'

Third Period : 1740-1800

The Rev. Josiah Thompson, junior (1724-1806), our chief authority on the state of Dissent in the latter half of the eighteenth century, was a Particular Baptist, who was minister of the Unicorn Yard church, 1746-1761, and a leading Nonconformist in London. His purpose in compiling a return in 1773, on lines similar to those of Evans in 1715, was to some extent political. He says : ' It is much to be wished some method could be thought of, for uniting the whole body of Dissenters—that in all public affairs we might act as one man, and be as wise in our Generation as the Quakers. . . . The Dissenting interest is perpetually changing and varying : and without a constant intercourse and correspondence kept up, we must always remain estranged to each other, and of course be unprepared to act upon any sudden emergency.' [1]

The Thompson List returns in 1773 for England (including Monmouth), 1,080 congregations, a decrease of nine on the Neal List and of twenty-four on that of Evans,

[1] MS. 'Records of Nonconformity,' No. 5—Dr. Williams's Library.

both of the year 1715.[1] The number of hearers cannot be compared as Thompson does not give such figures. This slight decrease in the number of congregations masks four important variations in the Dissenting interest. These are, a considerably larger relative decline; a decrease in the size of average congregations; a geographical variation in the distribution of Dissenters; and, Denominational variations.[2]

While we find the total number of congregations in 1773 only slightly less than in 1715, the population of the country had increased considerably during the intervening period, and therefore the relative decline was much greater. Then the large number of references in the reports made to Thompson, and incorporated in his MS., to the decline in individual congregations which were still in existence, point strongly to the likelihood that the average size of a Dissenting congregation had decreased since 1715. The following extracts from the MS. are given as illustrations of this tendency. The Rev. Mr. Chidlaw, of Chester, writes: 'The Dissenting Interest in this County in general is in a very declining, languishing state and some of the congregations likely to drop very soon,' while Mr. Berry, of Crediton, asserts his inability to 'find there is the least prospect of the revival of any Congregation in this County. But on the other hand it is almost certain that several . . . will shortly be no more.' This is from Devonshire, probably the County in which Dissent was strongest in 1715. It may have been an exaggeration due to the pessimism of the moment, and the comparative figures for 1715 and 1773, for Devonshire, do not suggest so bad a state of affairs, yet those figures are compatible with a large decrease in the size of congregations. It is a common experience that churches as corporate institutions have a considerable survival power although they easily fluctuate in membership. Similar stories are told in the MS. in respect of Derbyshire, Hampshire, Kent, Shropshire, Surrey, and Sussex. On the other hand, the correspondents in Leicestershire and Yorkshire report

[1] See Appendix II.
[2] These Denominational variations, interesting as they are, cannot be discussed here as they have no particular relevance to our main subject.

improvement, the latter giving fifteen new congregations as having arisen since 1745, of which nine were Baptist.

In regard to the geographical variation of Dissent, we find that the third quarter of the eighteenth century as compared with the first shows Dissent increasing nearly everywhere along a line drawn from Wiltshire almost due north to Northumberland, and with a notable increase in Lancashire, while south of a line drawn between London and Bristol, but excluding Wiltshire, there is an almost uninterrupted decrease.[1] This suggests that the movement of Dissent was to some extent, and in some areas, not unrelated to the Northern trend of population then obtaining.

For Wales, as already pointed out, both the Evans and Thompson Lists are rather uncertain, but apparently the year 1773 could show an increase over 1715 of forty-four Dissenting congregations, principally in the counties of Brecknockshire, Carmarthenshire, Cardiganshire, and Glamorganshire. During this period the Baptists report an increase of three congregations.[2] We have information, from separate sources, concerning the Particular Baptist churches in Wales in 1794, together with the date of the foundation of each, and the size of the membership in that year.[3] There were fifty-five churches for which figures are given, with an aggregate membership of 7,058, an average per congregation of 128. These churches were founded over a period of 161 years, the first dating from 1633, but slightly more than half the total began in the eighteen years between 1776 and 1794. It would appear from these two sets of figures that Dissent was spreading in Wales earlier than it revived in England; and, so far as the Baptists were concerned, the Particular Baptists were following rather than leading this forward movement.

Some evidence of the revival of Dissent and its steady growth in the last quarter of the eighteenth century, is supplied from the carefully kept statistics of the 'New Connexion of (Trinitarian) General (Arminian) Baptists.'[4]

[1] cf. figures by Counties given in Appendix II.   [1773.
[2] See Appendix III. No figures are available for Pembrokeshire for
[3] See Rippon: *The Baptist Annual Register*, 1794-1797.
[4] See Barclay: *The Inner Life of the Religious Societies of the Commonwealth*, Table 7.

With the exception of slight decreases in membership in the years 1779 and 1799, they record a steady increase from 1772 to the end of the century. In 1772, they had seven churches and in 1799, thirty-five with a membership of 3,385.

The history of individual churches, as well as the common reports of Church assemblies and leaders, illustrates the decline of Dissent during the first two or three quarters of the eighteenth century. In many cases, the churches gradually shrank, their influential members leaving or dying, and few arising to take their places, until finally the decease of the last influential supporter meant closing, or the decease or removal of the last minister had the same effect. In other cases, 'causes' were kept going only by help from central funds, or by the grouping of two or more churches for ministerial supply. The change in the state of Dissent between 1715 and 1773 is not only indicated by the figures given from the Evans, Neal, and Thompson Lists, but even more by a comparison of the footnotes and comments found in those documents. In 1715, there is abundant reference to the economic and social status of the Dissenters, and an obvious pride in their wealth and their influence in elections. In the 1773 List an altogether different atmosphere prevails. The aristocratic and wealthy supporters are very much less numerous, and Dissent for the most part is conscious of having its back to the wall in a long fight against indifference and stagnation.

We now come to a consideration of the statistics of Methodism.[1] The absolute accuracy of these statistics may be questioned—in the original printed copy of the Minutes in which they first appeared, they are sometimes inaccurately totalled—but as to their substantial accuracy there seems to be little doubt. These figures for Methodism present an almost uninterrupted story of growth, especially marked in 1778 and after, from which time most of the other Nonconformist bodies took a new lease of life.[2] The question arises as to whether this period of expansion on the part of Nonconformity generally was in any direct way due to the Methodist movement, a question of some importance here since the greater the influence of Methodism in the expansion

[1] See Appendix IV.   [2] cf. Appendix I.

of other Nonconformist bodies, the greater may have been its influence among them on social questions. Some writers argue against Methodist influence in this connexion, chiefly on the ground that the Methodist body was too small to influence greatly the much larger body of Dissenting churches.[1] In comparing the figures for Methodism, however, with those returned as 'hearers' in 1715, it should be borne in mind that the former do not include any but class-members,[2] whereas there were very considerable numbers who also came within the Methodist orbit. Neither do the Wesleyan figures cover the whole field of British Methodism, as there were in addition the followers of Whitefield, Howell Harris, and the Countess of Huntingdon.

The Thompson MS. gives some evidence of Methodist influence. The correspondent for Derbyshire writes of the Baptists of Melbourne : ' They have always been looked upon as Methodists but . . . they have now no manner of connexion with them.' We read of a body of Baptists and Paedobaptists at Greenwich who in 1771 'have separated themselves from the Methodists and united into a distinct society by themselves.' In Leicestershire, one of the counties from which better reports of the Dissenting interest had been received, we find ' in each of the above (i.e. fifteen) towns and villages there is started preaching every Lord's Day. These congregations, which are pretty considerable in point of numbers, were originally of the establishment, several of their present Pastors and other individuals now living received their first religious impressions from the preaching of Mr. Whitefield and Messrs. Wesley between thirty and forty years ago; not long after they formed themselves into little societies on the Methodistical Plan. . . . But . . . they never had any connexion with Mr. Whitefield or Messrs. Wesley.'

[1] As Fryer : *op. cit.,* p. 237—' The recovery was not due, as might be supposed, to Wesleyan influence, for the Wesleyan congregations numbered in 1770 only 25,000 hearers approximately.' Fryer does not distinguish between the different connotation of the term 'hearers' as used in the 1715 MS. and as applied to Methodism. Although Wesley himself often seriously over-estimated the number of his hearers, none the less Methodist congregations in the eighteenth century were frequently of remarkable size. Some, it is true, were drawn by curiosity or animosity, and cannot be reckoned as adherents.

[2] Wesley himself paid the utmost attention to having the lists of class-members quite accurate.

The Norfolk correspondent finds himself bound to reckon the Dissenting cause at Denton as ' rather among the Methodists than our Assemblies.' [1] In the earlier days of his itinerancy, Wesley often found that the Dissenting Ministers were as much opposed to him as the clergy of the Establishment, but later their opposition sensibly diminished, if it did not altogether cease. The difference in this respect between his earlier and his later tours is striking. Towards the end of his life as he progressed from place to place his reception was often a veritable triumph, an indication not only of his personal ascendency, but also of the spread and partial triumph of the body he had founded.

It seems possible that the following summary of the numbers of Nonconformists in the three periods reviewed may not be inaccurate, viz.,

1660-1700, between 150,000 and 250,000, the number rising from 1672 to the end of the century with occasional setbacks.

1700-1740, between 250,000 and 300,000, the maximum probably occurring before 1725, thereafter decreasing.

1740-1800, between 250,000 and 400,000 tending to rise throughout this period, especially towards the end of the century.[2]

These estimates, however, are of adults, so that a considerably larger number would have to be taken in order to estimate the proportion of the total population belonging to the Nonconformist tradition. On the other hand, it should not be forgotten that the population was increasing.[3]

[1] On the other hand, ' The revivals of Wesley and Whitefield scarcely touched the Friends : they were as suspicious of enthusiasm as a high Anglican . . .'—*Friends Historical Society,* V, p. 149.

[2] According to the 1801 Census, the accommodation in the chapels of the principal Nonconformist bodies provided seating for 868,374 persons. That the total number of adult adherents may have been only half the seating accommodation is by no means impossible.

[3] Nonconformity in Scotland, 1660-1800, was weak (the Scotch Presbyterians naturally cannot be counted as Nonconformists). In 1669 apparently there were only sixty-four male Quakers in all Scotland south of the River Tay, and in 1787, when another numbering took place, only twenty-three men and women were left, belonging to Edinburgh and Kelso, the sole surviving Meetings in the South of Scotland—see *F.H.S.,* I, p. 70. Methodism never got a strong foothold in Scotland. In 1773 there were 730 members only.

Chapter III

THE WEALTH AND INFLUENCE OF NONCONFORMISTS

The social and economic importance of Nonconformity to the nation at large is certain to be directly related to the social and economic status of individual Nonconformists. We must, therefore, inquire what proportion of their numbers belonged to the working-classes, and whether that proportion increased or decreased during the period. We must ask if amongst the classes of the landed gentry and tradesmen, respectively, Nonconformity maintained or varied its hold, and if the general level of wealth amongst the Nonconformists was rising or falling. In discussing these and similar questions it will be found convenient to consider separately the three periods, 1660-1700, 1700-1740, and 1740-1800, distinguished in the previous chapter.

First Period: 1660-1700

A number of the early Quakers were known as 'The First Publishers of Truth,' and were itinerating in 1654 as preachers. These were followed by others in succeeding years. Of the earlier of these itinerants, the occupations of fifty-three of the men are known: thirty-eight were closely connected with agriculture, five of whom were gentlemen; seven were engaged in trade; and eight were in the professions, two being soldiers. Of seven women who were amongst them, two were wives of yeomen, and one a sister; one was the wife of a shopkeeper; one the sister of a crafts-man; and two were serving maids. Of the main body of these itinerants, the occupations are known in 125 cases, men and women: seventy-four were engaged in agriculture, twelve being gentlemen; twenty-eight were engaged in trade; and twenty-three in the professions.[1] Of these early Quaker

[1] *F.H.S.*, 1922, pp. 66-81.

leaders, we thus find out of 185, seventeen were landed gentlemen, and ninety-eight otherwise concerned in agriculture; thirty-seven were in trade; thirty-one connected with the professions; and two were serving maids.

Amongst those early touched by the Quakers was Lady Margaret Hambleton, who was convinced in 1657,[1] and William Penn, who became a convinced Quaker in 1667 and one of the foremost leaders of that body. He was the son of an Admiral, and like his father a personal friend of James II.[2] The distraints made on the Quakers as a result of their resistance to tithes indicates that many of them were substantial men. A large proportion of them were of yeoman origin,[3] with some gentry and merchants, also artisans and labourers. The Friends' General Meeting of Dublin, in 1686 and 1693 shows that amongst their people were tailors, joiners, ships-carpenters, brass-founders, saddlers, and shoemakers. In 1680 we learn that there were also manufacturers of linen and woollen goods connected with them. The regulations made by Friends in different parts of England for the right prosecution of trade suggest that in the period at the end of the seventeenth and at the beginning of the eighteenth century, they had many traders and shopkeepers amongst their adherents.[4] In this period Bristol was one of the strongholds of the Quakers, and Minute-books show the standing of their members to have varied somewhat. On the one hand there are mentioned carpenters, bakers, tobacco-cutters, butchers, tailors, apothecaries, gallipot-makers, grocers, wool-combers, soap-boilers, shoe-makers, silk-weavers, gunsmiths and tilers. On the other hand, a wealthier status is indicated by a Minute of 1699 which censured 'Friends' coaches' driving up to the meeting-house—they should 'stay in the street, as some have been hurt.'[5]

The Quakers in Wales in the seventeenth century included a labourer, a hatter, a doctor, a shoe-maker, some justices of the peace, and several substantial farmers. Twenty-three people arrested at a meeting near Dolgellau in 1660, for

[1] George Fox: *Journal*, I, p. 394.
[2] See Graham: *William Penn Founder of Pennsylvania.*
[3] Braithwaite: *Beginnings of Quakerism*, p. 512.
[4] Robert Barclay: *The Inner Life of the Religious Societies of the Commonwealth*, pp. 492f.   [5] *ibid.*, pp. 322f.

example, had between them more than 600 cattle and beasts. Of these substantial farmers a number belonged to the gentry, being of known and distinguished lineage.[1]

The records of the Edinburgh Meeting—covering all South Scotland—from 1656 to about 1790, give the occupations of some of the Friends, which show there to have been within this period, nineteen gardeners and seedsmen, nineteen weavers, ten male and female servants, ten shopkeepers, six tanners, six tailors, five glovers, four shoe-makers, three brewers, three bleachers, three tobacco-merchants, three linen-drapers, two doctors, two smiths and farriers, two skippers, two wrights, two school-mistresses, two dyers, two hatters, a stocking-maker, cooper, coal-grieve, coach-driver, printer, clothier, sieve-wright, inn-keeper, and a steward; there were five small landed proprietors and perhaps only three 'lairds.'[2]

In the last forty years of the seventeenth century there were many within the ranks of Dissent who belonged to the gentry, and were wealthy, some belonging to the nobility, too. In an account of Conventicles in London, of 1664 it is reported that the Countesses of Valentia, Peterborough and Anglesey, and 'others of quality,' were present at a Dissenters' meeting, a former justice of the peace offering prayer.[3] The ministers silenced by the Act of Uniformity were, in many cases, befriended by members of the nobility, especially by ladies of rank, notable amongst whom was the Dowager Countess of Exeter.[4] Lady Hewley, a personal friend of the well-known Presbyterian, Oliver Heywood, was a munificent benefactor of contemporary Dissent, and generally speaking we find the Presbyterians to have been of a higher social status than members of the other Dissenting bodies. Another of Heywood's friends, a powerful Dissenter, living in the Silk-stone and Penistone district of Yorkshire, was William Cotton, a great ironmaster.[5] Amongst the most influential London Presbyterians in 1672, were three wealthy brewers,

[1] Richard Jones: *Crynwyr Bore Cymru* (Early Quakers of Wales), pp. 21, 30, 37, 39, 42, 53, 56, 59, 60, 67f, 81, 84, 90, 115.
[2] *F.H.S.*, I, pp. 69f.
[3] *C.S.P.D.*, 1663-1664, p. 678.
[4] Neal: *History of the Puritans*, V, p. 45.
[5] Hunter: *The Rise of the Old Dissent*, p. 270. Also, Ashton, T. S.: *Iron and Steel in the Industrial Revolution*, p. 213 (footnote).

partners, named Bull, Mays, and Stancliffe, each of whom was a preacher.[1] Many of the merchants of the great city companies were Presbyterian, and after the ejectment of 1662, the city companies leased their halls to the Presbyterians for worship. Sir John Shorter, a Presbyterian, was Lord Mayor during an indulgent period of James II's reign. Almost at the end of the century, the then Lord Mayor, Sir Humphrey Edwin, another Presbyterian, created considerable opposition by carrying the regalia of his office to the Meeting-house held at Pinners' Hall.[2] Sir Thomas Abney was a third Presbyterian to hold this office at that period, in 1701.

On several occasions the Baptists arranged with the Presbyterians for the partial and temporary use of leased company halls. Amongst the halls so used were those of the Brewers, Curriers, Glaziers, Glovers, Joiners, Loriners, Pinners, Slaters, Tallow-chandlers, and Turners. One only of these, however, concerned the General Baptists—the Glaziers' Hall used in 1649—a sign perhaps of their poverty.[3] One of the most influential Baptists of this period in London was Kiffin, a Particular Baptist, who was an Alderman and Justice, although he 'never meddled with either of those places.'[4] Kiffin was a merchant, influential both with Cromwell and Charles II. He offered evidence to a House of Commons Committee, and subsequently before the Council, against the monopoly of the export of woollen cloths being given to the Hamburg Company. Most of the Baptists, however, seem to have been of the poorer classes, labourers, tailors, shopkeepers, bakers, yeomen, some farmers, with only occasionally a landed gentleman.[5]

In the ranks of the Independents there were to be found men and women of position. Records of the Mark Lane Independent church show that in 1673 the membership included 'Lord' Charles Fleetwood, the son-in-law of Oliver Cromwell; Sir John and Lady Hartopp; Mr. and Mrs. Fleetwood, Mrs. Fleetwood having been Bridget Cromwell;

[1] *C.H.S.*, III, p. 198.
[2] Toulmin: *An Historical View . . . Dissenters*, p. 120.
[3] *Baptist Minutes*, introduction by Whitley, II, p. 16.
[4] *Life of Kiffin* by Himself, p. 87.
[5] *Baptist Minutes*, Introduction, I, pp. 42-48. One Taverner was a grocer about 1670 who had been Governor of Deal Castle from 1652 to 1665.

Wm. Steele, Sergt.-at-law; Col. John Desborough, Cromwell's brother-in-law; Dr. Wm. Staines; Col. Berry; Col. Ellistone; Mrs. Bendish, grand-daughter of Cromwell; Capt. Lloyd; Lady Vere Wilkinson; Lady Dethick. In 1675 Sir Thomas Overbury became a member, and the Countess of Anglesey five years later.[1]

Second Period : 1700-1740

The Quakers in the early eighteenth century were closely connected with the iron industry in all the ironfields of the country. Most notable was the 'Darby dynasty' of Coalbrookdale in Shropshire, each of the three Abraham Darbys being a devout Quaker, married to a Quaker woman. Other important Quaker ironmasters were Rawlinson of Backbarrow; Charles Lloyd of Dolobran; John Pemberton and Isaac Spooner of Birmingham; Richard Parkes and John and Samuel Fidoe of Wednesbury; Booth Hodgetts of Dudley; Gardner, Manser and Co. of Rotherhithe. Amongst the Sheffield steel makers were the Huntsmans and Doncasters. Many of these Quaker families intermarried.[2]

For the Dissenters, the Evans MS. is the principal source for this period.[3] In the case of some counties the information is full, details being given for every, or almost every church; in others only a sparse amount of information is available; and for some, none. The total numbers actually recorded are :

ENGLAND (including Monmouth)

	Esquires	Gentlemen	Tradesmen	Yeomen and Farmers	Labourers
	39	1,394	1,662	1,631	1,419
WALES					
	2	9	51	167	210

Unfortunately, amongst the counties for which little or no information of this sort is given are Middlesex (including part of London), Devonshire, Lancashire, Somersetshire, Suffolk, and Yorkshire—counties in which Dissent was strong. Hence it is certain that the number of gentlemen and other prosperous adherents should be considerably greater than that

[1] *C.H.S.,* I, pp. 27-30.
[2] Ashton, T. S.: *Iron and Steel in the Industrial Revolution,* p. 211.
[3] Appendices V and VI summarize the information concerning the Dissenters' social and economic status, for England and Wales respectively.

given, yet enough is given to show that in 1715 Dissent could number many influential and wealthy supporters. There is no mention, however, of men of title, with one exception at Hand Alley, London, where a baronet is referred to. It is possible that there may have been some such in the counties for which information is lacking, but the suggestion seems reasonable that the preceding quarter of a century or so had seen a decline in the support of Dissent among the aristocracy which was before long to be reflected in the growing secession of the gentry. A comparison of Appendices II and V shows that the following counties were relatively strong in the number of landed gentlemen who were Dissenters, viz. Cheshire, Cornwall, Essex, Lincolnshire, Nottinghamshire, Rutlandshire, Westmoreland. The following counties were, compared with the total number of Dissenters and churches, strong in the trading interest, viz. Berkshire, Cheshire, Cornwall, Monmouthshire, Nottinghamshire, Shropshire. If fuller information were available, however, probably other counties would have to be added to these lists.

In two important cases, Hand Alley church, Bishopsgate Street, London, and the Bristol churches, full information is separately given in the Evans MS. Hand Alley was a Presbyterian church of 1,000 hearers, of which the wealthy educationalist and philanthropist, Dr. Daniel Williams had been the minister, followed by John Evans, the compiler of this MS., who was ordained in 1702. In 1715 this church had amongst its membership one Baronet, one Esquire, eight men worth £10,000 or upwards, forty-three 'men of substance,' fifty-five who were voters for Magistrates, fifty-four Liverymen of London, twenty-six Freeholders (some of whom were freeholders in more than one county), six voters in other Corporations, viz. Coventry, Norwich, Blechingley, Ryegate, Southwark (two).

In the case of Bristol, there are five churches which are not named territorially, but are given separately under the names of their respective ministers. The first church had about 500 hearers. 'Very few of them poor. The whole congregation is reckoned worth £100,000.' The second church numbered about 1,600 hearers. 'Some have been sheriffs of the city and put themselves out of the Council because of the Occasional Act[1] . . . few poor. The whole congregation computed worth near £400,000.' The third could muster 500 hearers. 'Worth between £60,000 and £70,000.' The fourth had 1,200 hearers. 'Worth about £160,000.' The last churches numbered between 400 and 500, 'worth about £50,000.' These figures give a total for Bristol of 4,300 hearers, worth £770,000, which yields an average of almost £180 per head, a truly remarkable figure. The care and detail in the MS. encourage faith in the substantial accuracy of these figures. A note informs us that 'many of them also as merchants pay large sums yearly for customs to the Crown. Many others are great promoters of the woollen manufacture. And several have estates fit for Justice of the Peace.' A comment is also made on the Quakers in Bristol: ' (they) are generally well-affected to the present government, large traders and very rich. Their number may be supposed about 2,000 and upwards; and their wealth not less than £500,000.' ' And the strength of all the Dissenters in Bristol may justly be reckoned much more than that of all the Low Church Party there.'

From the information given in this MS. it would appear that Dissent in 1715, though principally among the poorer classes, had considerable support among the gentry, many adherents amongst tradesmen and farmers, and some very wealthy members. Dissenters also had a considerable power through their votes.[2] In London and Bristol there was much wealth among them, also in parts of the counties of Cumberland, Essex, Monmouthshire, Hampshire, Surrey, Sussex, and Wiltshire. In Wales, Monmouth excluded, only two Esquires and nine gentlemen are reported, as we have seen, but there are considerable lacunae in the information given.

A list of Baptist Ministers in London for 1709-1719 was compiled, which in some cases gives their trades, viz. Burch, hatter; Thomas Congrove, tailor; Nathanael Foxwell, butcher; Joseph Jenkins, ribbon-weaver; Caleb Langford, tallow-chandler; John Maulden, shoe-maker; Abraham Mulliner, tailor.[3] We also know of a Baptist minister of

---

1 i.e. the Occasional Conformity Act, 1711. 2 See pp. 82f *infra*.
3 *Baptist Minutes*, I, p. 100.

Harringworth who combined the occupations of carpenter and
farmer with that of preacher. Richard Haines,[1] of Horsham,
Sussex, was a wealthy farmer, merchant and inventor. The
low economic status of the Baptists, generally, appears in
1710, when an appeal for a central fund by the General
Baptists suggests that members shall give ' weekly a farthing
or half-penny or more as they think fit.' [2] There were some
Baptists, however, of a different stamp. Whiston, Professor
of Mathematics at Cambridge, was expelled as holding
unorthodox views, who later became a General Baptist.[3]

THIRD PERIOD : 1740-1800

The social and economic importance of Dissent in this
period had considerably shrunk from that of the earlier
periods. The artisan, tradesman, and labourer were in a
greater majority than formerly. Dissent had lost much of its
fervour and its earlier uncompromising character. It had
gained somewhat in ' respectability,' but in that it could not
hope to compete with the Anglican Church, and we find the
gentry becoming, nominally at least, Anglicans. In the case
of Methodism, very few of its adherents were socially
distinguished, or possessed of much wealth, prior to their
joining these new societies. On the other hand, there were
many of its poorer members who rapidly became much better
off, but although they soon began to acquire some economic
importance, yet social distinction, in its narrower sense, they
hardly acquired at all.

The Wesleys did not attract the aristocrat as did Whitefield,
for whom the Countess of Huntingdon used to arrange
meetings to which members of the nobility and gentry came,
sometimes in large numbers. It was the man who came from
the humble home, Whitefield, who could attract the high-born
whom the aristocratic Wesleys failed for the most part to
touch, even where they did not antagonize.[4] Amongst the
few aristocrats who either became Methodists, or were in
close touch and sympathy with Methodism, in addition to the

[1] On Haines, see pp. 61f. and 129f. *infra.*
[2] *Baptist Minutes,* I, p. 110.   [3] Dale : *op. cit.,* pp. 531f.
[4] Perhaps because of his humbler origin, Whitefield set a higher value
on rank and social distinction than did Wesley, aristocratic and autocratic
as the latter naturally was.

Countess of Huntingdon, were the Earl and Countess of Buchan, Lady Maxwell, Lady Ann Erskine, Lady Spencer, and Lady Glenorchy. In 1741, Lady Mary Hastings married the preacher Ingham, while Lord Bath attended Whitefield's Tabernacle. It was inevitable that for the most part Wesley's converts should be from the poorer strata of society because of the reputation he earned as an ' enthusiast ' in the eyes of the well-to-do. Also, the opposition of the Anglican clergy, which became widespread when once they realized what kind of man and message it was with which they had to deal, would act as an effectual social barrier in many quarters for a long while. Yet it must be said that Wesley's *Journal* reveals more than 200 Anglican clergymen, at one time or another, manifesting practical sympathy with his work.

The economic and social position of Wesley's almost constantly growing band of preachers, which by 1767 totalled over 100, and had passed the 500 mark by the end of the century, is important. At first, any one who became a preacher went out in faith, whether married or single. ' In those days we had no provision made for preachers' wives, no funds, no stewards. He that had a staff might take it, go without, or stay at home.' [1] So wrote one of them. That Methodism was a great social force in the eighteenth century is hardly to be denied, although opinion may vary as to how great, but it is amazing how slight was its financial cost. At first, preachers were not permitted to receive money, although they might accept food and clothing. In 1752, £12 p.a. was allowed each preacher, the stewards previously having supplied their bare needs. In 1765, at the Manchester Conference, we find the York Circuit appealing ' against the large sum of £12 a year for the preachers,' [2] but it was continued, and at the end of the century increased by £4 p.a. The first allowance

---

[1] *Preachers*, I, p. 200.
[2] *New History of Methodism*, I, pp. 303f. The Bradford Circuit Book, in 1770, illustrates the usage of the times, viz.,

	£	s.	d.
Preacher's quarterly board, 13 weeks @ 3/6 ...	2	5	6
Preacher's quarterage	3	0	0
Preacher's quarterage for wife	1	17	6
Allowed for servant		12	6
Allowed for turnpikes		6	0
	8	1	6

for a preacher's wife was that paid to Mrs. Mather, in London, of 4s. per week, which began in 1757, but in Ireland in 1768, ' Mrs. Taylor received £4 or four guineas for the whole year.' [1] The year following, 1769, Conference fixed the allowance of a preacher's wife at £10 p.a. The Worn-Out Preachers' Fund was begun in 1763, but although conditions improved for the preachers, they remained very poor indeed, unless they had private means. ' It is not surprising that some of the preachers followed a trade . . . or carried medicine, &c., for sale. It soon became apparent that this was highly inexpedient, and it was forbidden (1768).' [2]

The economic position of the preachers was not without its influence on the success of Wesley's movement. The early converts were not burdened to provide for their ministers, while on the other hand they saw poor men, often of great natural ability, and sometimes of considerable education, voluntarily adopt a very real poverty for their benefit. This fact of voluntary poverty was a powerful appeal to those who were involuntarily poor. It was also part of a general policy or principle, that preachers ought to be poor men, not on ascetic grounds, but because the needs of the poor round about ought to keep them poor by the call on their charity. Socially, the position of the Methodist preachers differed somewhat from their economic position. After a few years many of them obtained a very great influence amongst the growing number of the followers of Wesley. They became social as well as spiritual forces amongst their congregations. Their personal social background was very varied. A number had been, or still were, clergymen of the State Church, some schoolmasters, others from most of the ordinary occupations. Peter Jaco was a Cornish pilchard fisherman converted by the preaching of Stephen Nichols, a tinner; John Nelson was a stonemason; Thomas Olivers was apprenticed to a shoe-maker; Thomas Walsh was a schoolmaster; while several, such as Haime, had been soldiers.

---

[1] *Wesley Historical Society Proceedings*, VIII, p. 181.

[2] Down to the present century, the remuneration of Methodist ministers has been regarded, not as salary, but as ' maintenance.' In the eighteenth century this maintenance was so low that it is not surprising to find that many of the early preachers died young, and more than half of them soon ceased to itinerate—see *N.H.M.*, I, p. 304.

A fragment, in Wesley's handwriting, dated January 1, 1741, gives the names and occupations of some of the early members of The United Bristol Society, viz. Richard Cross, upholsterer; John Deschamps, stuff-maker; Capt. Joseph Turner, mariner; John Alldin, cordwainer; Thomas Gough, freeholder; Wm. Phillips, glassmaker; James Kelson, cordwainer; Wm. Martin, house carpenter; John Tripp, gunsmith.[1] The Class Register of Newlands, near Newcastle, apparently in Wesley's handwriting, gives the names of forty-four persons, including boys, whose ages are given as twelve, thirteen, and seventeen, and a girl of fourteen. These represent twenty-two families, fourteen of which were farmers, two weavers, and one family represented each of the following occupations—miller, smith, servant, labourer, tailor, harvester.[2] From the Grimsby Circuit Registers, it appears that in 1784, in the Raithby Society, one class had twenty-one members representing sixteen families. Of these one was classified as esquire, two gentlewomen, one captain, three farmers, four spinsters, one gardener, one cutler, two labourers and one servant.[3]

Sometimes we find, it is true, richer people amongst Wesley's congregations. There are, for instance, two references in his *Journal* in the spring of 1758 to the presence of rich and genteel hearers—at Liverpool and Portarlington. But Wesley's own comments show that he did not expect much good to be done amongst such. As the Industrial Revolution got into its stride, iron-masters, cotton manufacturers, and others, are not infrequently found in the Methodist ranks, some of them having risen from comparative poverty.[4] As this occurred, a social differentiation sometimes became evident in the new chapels which were built. There had always been the possibility of this, but against it Wesley set his face. As early as 1744, we find him writing in a letter: ' we have no 5s. or 2s. 6d. places at the Foundery, nor ever had, nor ever will. If any one asks me for a place in the gallery . . . he has it; I refuse none. And some hundreds have places there

---

[1] *W.H.S.*, IV, pp. 94-96.   [2] *ibid*, XII, pp. 76f.   [3] *ibid*, XIII, p. 69.
[4] Ashton, T. S.: *op. cit.*, p. 221. The important Masborough Walkers, ironmasters, were Methodists, as were all the partners in the big Thorncliffe ironworks. Almost all the South Wales iron-masters, except Richard Crayshaw, were Methodists, notably the Guests.

who pay nothing at all.   First come also is first served, at every time of preaching.   And the poorest have frequently the best places, because they come first.' [1]

The foregoing evidence on the wealth and social influence of Nonconformists indicates an important trend.   In the years following the ejectment of ministers in 1662, we find that Nonconformity included some members of the aristocracy, many of the gentry and local magnates, and many engaged in trade, large and small, as well as numerous labourers and workmen.   This statement applies, in a greater or lesser degree, to Presbyterians, Independents, and Quakers, but not to the Baptists who were, with some few exceptions, of the economically inferior classes.   By the beginning of the eighteenth century, however, few members of the nobility could be found amongst the Nonconformists, and by 1740 the number of Nonconformists amongst the gentry had sensibly diminished.   They were still, at this time, quite important in trade, with many wealthy, but this importance was soon rapidly to shrink.   So, by a process of attrition, first the socially distinguished, then the economically powerful sections of early Nonconformity almost disappeared, having been for the most part re-absorbed into the Anglican Communion. Then arose the new Nonconformity, Methodism, which started socially and economically from the bottom, and before the nineteenth century had dawned had sprung into some economic importance although it had little social prominence. Established wealth and position is rarely for long at home in English Protestant Nonconformity.   On the other hand, we find, historically, that one of the types of persons to whom this Nonconformity appeals tends to become wealthy by a personal endeavour and abstinence encouraged by this type of Christianity.

---

[1] *Letters*, II, p. 25.

Chapter IV

NONCONFORMIST CHURCH DISCIPLINE

THE social effectiveness of a Church will depend in part on the nature and severity of the discipline exercised by it over its members. We have, then, to ask if the Nonconformist bodies put any outward constraints upon their members to conform to a recognized standard of conduct, and if so, to what extent they succeeded in their object. We must especially inquire if they attempted anything in the nature of an economic supervision of their adherents. And first we shall notice that the Nonconformist organization was more democratic and called for a greater degree of individual initiative than did that of the State Church. This democratic element in Church life could make either for freedom or for regulation. On the one hand, economic life might free itself from Church interference through the greater initiative of members. On the other, a minute supervision of the economic and social life of the individual might be attempted. Actually, we can find both of these contrary tendencies at work. It ought, however, to be remembered that the teaching and views of a body are likely to create an outlook and a tradition which in itself would make it difficult for members of that body to act otherwise, consequently we shall not be surprised to find cases of discipline to be comparatively rare. In the economic sphere, the most striking and thorough attempt at oversight is that supplied by the Quakers, of which a number of illustrations will now be given.

The London Yearly Meeting of 1675 advised all Quakers in their respective Meetings to ' watch over one another in the love of God . . . particularly admonishing that none trade beyond their ability nor stretch beyond their compass; and that they use few words in their dealings, and keep their word in all things.' In 1688, warning was given lest Friends, taking advantage of the cessation of persecution should allow themselves to embark on business affairs greater than they

could sustain. The same Meeting, in 1692, was against delay
in the due discharge of debts, or incurring over large debts,
and warned members not ' to break their promises, contracts,
or agreements, in their buying or selling.'   Further, those
about to begin trading, or those traders who had insufficient
stock, should ' be very cautious of running themselves into
debt, without advising some of their experienced Friends.' [1]

In 1678 the Cork Three Weeks Meeting appointed some
of their number ' to speak with ye friends of the Cloathing
or Spinning trade that they take care in all theire dealings
with spinners and other folkes, to pay either money for their
worke or such goods as they shall fully agree for before hand,
and to desire if they pay goods it may not be allowed above
ye Current price.' [2]   Here we have an early example of an
attempt to deal with abuses of the truck system of payment.
The Dublin Yearly Meeting of 1680 decided against Friends
moving from one place to another, unless with the Church's
sanction.[3]   The Half-yearly Meeting, also at Dublin, in 1702,
laid it down that ' manufacturers of linen and woollen goods
were to make their goods honest and substantial,' and since
there were great complaints that such goods were ' often made
slightly, and so of little service to the wearer,' guilty parties
who persisted in ' refractory non-compliance,' were to be
excommunicated.[4]   At the same time the question of the
financial soundness of Friends came up, and so ' a strict and
diligent inspection into the condition and circumstance of all
Friends ' was ordered if there was ground to suspect un-
soundness, and such persons were to supply full and accurate
information as to their capital, debts, and creditors.[5]

In Bristol, about this time, it was proposed, to be carried
forward through the Quarterly to the Yearly Meeting, that
every Meeting should appoint two or three people to whom
each member must give an account of his financial position
and standard of living, with the object of avoiding business
failures.   The Quarterly Meeting, however, dropped this
drastic proposal,[6] which none the less indicates the disciplinary

---

[1] Society of Friends : *The Book of Christian Discipline*, pp. 117f.
[2] *F.H.S.*, 1915, p. 52.
[3] Robert Barclay : *Religious Societies of the Commonwealth*, p. 493.
[4] *ibid*, pp. 493f.
[5] and [6] *ibid*, p. 494.

attitude of the day, and is especially significant as coming from Bristol, where so many Quakers lived who were rich traders. The Hardshaw Quarterly Meeting, in 1697, decided on the continuance of an inquiry and inspection into the business affairs of all their members, but with the chief object in this case of ensuring that the members were not becoming too worldly.[1] The same Meeting, in 1703, laid down the questions that should be asked on such an inspection : 1st. Dost thou undertake more concerns and business in the world than thou canst respectably manage with respect to thy profession? . . . Art thou concerned to serve Truth with thy substance? 2nd. Art thou capable, by thy undertakings, to supply thy family; to maintain a reputable and solid credit? Art thou content with thy station without seeking great things beyond thy compass? 3rd. Dost thou endeavour to keep thyself from being burdensome to any? Dost thou labour according to thy ability, and not eat the bread of idleness nor live of the labour of others whilst able to do for thyself?'[2]

The London Yearly Meeting of 1771 sent out an Epistle in which accommodation bills and suretyships were dealt with. The former were strongly condemned, being termed 'an appearance of value without an intrinsic reality.' The latter, while not condemned forthright, were considered to be dangerous. 'We would caution Friends against imprudently entering into joint securities with others; by which many innocent wives and children have been inevitably and unexpectedly involved in ruinous and deplorable circumstances.'[3]

Strict discipline seems to have been usual in the early part of our period amongst the Baptists, although it was not often shown in social and economic matters, probably because they were the poorest of the Dissenting bodies. In 1666, the Particular Baptists in London, Kiffin's congregation, ejected a young man who had misrepresented his financial position in order to secure a bride of a higher social class.[4] The records of the Hanserd Knollys church, Thames Street, London, a

---

[1] Robert Barclay : *Religious Societies of the Commonwealth*, pp. 494f, footnote.   [2] *ibid*, ditto.
[3] Society of Friends : *Book of Christian Discipline*, p. 119.
[4] Whiting : *Studies in English Puritanism from the Restoration to the Revolution*, p. 96.

decade later, give an illustration of discipline being enforced against an apprentice, charged by his master, a scrivener, with negligence, disobedience, and insubordination. The apprentice repented, but was again charged, and then excluded.[1] The Lincolnshire General Baptist Association posed two questions to the General Assembly in 1711. The first concerned playing cards, and it was decided that to persist ' therein in opposition in contempt of all Christian council and advice to the contrary is unbecoming and unlawful for such as profess the Gospel of Christ and unfits them for Church communion.' The second question concerned ministerial conduct in particular. Lincolnshire wanted to know what attitude to take in regard to a minister who practised or contended for dancing, cock-fighting, and ' many other vices although being moderately used.' [2] The Assembly ruled that such a man was disqualified from both the ministerial office and Church communion, until he had made a satisfactory repentance. However, the same question cropped up from the same quarter sixty years later, when the Assembly passed a tame resolution, ' We declare no such encouragement is given for the practice countenanced by any Minister or Ministers amongst us.' [3] The strictness of the Baptists was going, and a little later their attitude openly changed, for in 1780 a Minute of this Assembly reiterated a conviction of the wrongfulness of gambling, but definitely disowned any right of prying into private lives,[4] an attitude different from that of the Quakers and the Methodists.

It is significant of the changed attitude of the Baptists, that with one exception, the General Baptist Minutes, extending over the whole period 1660-1800, can produce no other illustration of discipline in regard to social or economic matters, and that the one just given should be of so trivial a character, and apparently regarded also as trivial. The one exception is of some importance and concerns an eminent Baptist, Richard Haines, who belonged to Horsham. He was able and wealthy, a writer on poor law and the employment of the poor,[5] a farmer, manufacturer and inventor. Haines applied for a patent for a process he had discovered

[1] *Baptist Quarterly*, Vol. I, No. 3, pp. 112-128, and No. 4, pp. 179-185. (Reprint of Book of Discipline kept by Robert Steed, 1689-1699.)
[2] *Baptist Minutes*, I, p. 115.
[3] *ibid*, II, p. 143.   [4] *ibid*, II, p. 169.   [5] See *infra*, pp. 129f.

experimentally of cleaning trefoil so as to improve the seed. Matthew Caffin was then pastor of the Horsham church, a man of very considerable influence in contemporary Baptist circles, whose views on patents were perhaps not uninfluenced by some jealousy of Haines, as the latter was on friendly terms with many of the notable people in the district. Caffin summoned Haines to discuss in Church-meeting whether patents were allowable to a Christian. His own view, not unlike that of the Levellers of the previous century, was that patentees were covetous and to be classified with idolators and unclean persons. A second meeting became somewhat disorderly. Caffin then excommunicated Haines on the ground that his greed was causing a general scandal in the country, and reflecting on the Church. Haines now carried the matter formally to the Assembly, which considered it in 1673, but apparently in an inconclusive way. He lodged a second appeal the following year, and the controversy dragged on until 1680, when the Assembly reversed the excommunication and ordered Caffin to rescind it, which he promised to do.[1]

Examples of discipline in cases of drunkenness were not uncommon amongst the Dissenters. Several early examples are to be found in the records of the Broadmead (Bristol) Baptist church. In May, 1670, one Philip Sciphard was excluded, while in January, 1676/77, Tho. Jacob was admonished, also for drunkenness, only to be excluded rather more than a year later. Jeremy Courtney was admonished before the Church for this offence in March, 1678, but was again drunk before the month was out. The Church therefore held a day of solemn fasting and prayer with the object of casting out the 'drunken devil.' Apparently this succeeded in effecting his reformation for we hear no more about him.[2] This attitude on the part of the Baptists towards drunkenness amongst their members seems to have been usual and to have persisted. Nearly a century later, in 1773, the Minutes of the Monthly Conferences of the Ministers of the Leicestershire New Connexion of General Baptists, record the following decision: 'It was agreed that Bro. Wyatt should

---

[1] *Baptist Minutes,* Introduction to Vol. II, pp. 12-14.
[2] *The Records of a Church of Christ, meeting in Broadmead, Bristol,* 1640-1687, pp. 107, 363-5, 379, 384-7.

be privately admonished for drinking to axcess (sic) and
afterwards brought to the Church to confess the crime, and
to be restored, provided the Church be satisfied with his
conviction and repentance.'[1]   The records of Congrega-
tionalism in the Fen Country reveal that about 1695, one
Richard Chest of Reach was ejected ' for public and gross
Drunkenness, being mad drunk.'[2]   In 1697 a man named
Ward, after being warned over a considerable period, was
excluded for gross drunkenness.[3]   One John Hunt was excommunicated in 1702 for gross drunkenness, swearing and
fighting.[4]   Quakers were advised by their Yearly Meeting in
1751 to be carefully and cautiously temperate in their consumption of alcoholic beverages.   An Epistle of 1797 warned
Friends against remaining in public houses ' after the purpose
of business or refreshment is accomplished.'[5]

Congregational discipline in the Fen Country was also
shown in some other aspects of social life.   In 1704 a man
named Edward Smit (sic) of Burwel was put out for
deserting his wife and child.   In 1712, a woman named Fisher
was excommunicated for perjury, and in 1715, John Watson
and his wife for ' their scandalous living in fighting.'[6]   It
seems that in the Fen Country conduct was lax and that the
Congregational Churches were determined to fight it.   In
1707, they engaged in ' A Solemn Renewal of Covenant . . .
we will submit to, and use . . . the censures of Reproof,
Admonition, and excommunication,' to show they would not
have in their churches those whose manner of life seemed
to them to be unworthy.[7]

Turning to Methodist discipline, we find it concerned more
with moral and social faults than ecclesiastical.   Wesley was
an autocrat who demanded that his ' Assistants' should
exercise on his behalf an autocracy in their several districts.[8]
He believed in the detailed investigation of each individual into
everything in his life, and in the hardly less detailed investigation of others into the life of each individual.   It is true that

---

[1] *Baptist Historical Society,* Vol. V, No. 1, p. 40.
[2] *C.H.S.,* Vol. VI, p. 422.
[3] *ibid,* Vol. VI, pp. 424f.   [4] *ibid,* Vol. VII, p. 4.
[5] Society of Friends : *Book of Christian Discipline,* p. 107.
[6] *C.H.S.,* Vol. VII, pp. 5 and 11.   [7] *ibid,* Vol. VII, p. 6.
[8] ' And remember !   A Methodist preacher is to mind every point, great
and small, in the Methodist discipline.'—*N.H.M.,* I, p. 296.

this ideal was never universally practised, and in some districts, at times, was temporarily lost sight of. Nevertheless, it was an ideal laboriously sought and in many cases rigorously enforced. Wesley very early instituted the ' Bands,' in which the most earnest of his followers were to be found. On December 25, 1738, he drew up a remarkable document entitled, ' Rules of the Band Societies.' In this he says : ' The design of our meeting is, to obey that command of God, " Confess your faults one to another, and pray for one another, that ye may be healed." ' He would not admit to the Bands any who were in doubt as to what was involved, and hence certain questions were to be put to each candidate, in which occurred the following : ' Do you desire to be told of all your faults, and that plain and home? . . . Consider! Do you desire we should tell you whatsoever we think, whatsoever we fear, whatsoever we hear, concerning you? Do you desire that, in doing this, we should come as close as possible, that we should cut to the quick, and search your heart to the bottom? Is it your desire and design to be on this, and all other occasions, entirely open, so as to speak everything that is in your heart without exception, without disguise, and without reserve? ' [1]

Exactly six years later, Wesley issued his ' Directions given to the Band Societies.' He writes : ' You are supposed to have the faith that " overcometh the world." To you, therefore, it is not grievous, Carefully to abstain from doing evil; in particular (*inter alia*) To taste no spirituous liquor, no dram of any kind, unless prescribed by a Physician. To be at a word in buying and selling. To pawn nothing, no not to save life. To wear no needless ornaments, such as rings, ear-rings. To use no needless self-indulgence, such as taking snuff or tobacco, unless prescribed by a Physician . . . To give alms of such things as you possess, and that to the uttermost of your power. To be patterns of diligence and frugality, of self-denial, and taking up the cross daily.' [2] In short, members of the Bands were to have their whole lives brought under minute and constant scrutiny, not only in

[1] *Works*, VIII, pp. 272f.
[2] *ibid*, VIII, pp. 273f. For the similar Rules of the United Societies, see *N.H.M.*, II, pp. 563-5 (Appendix D).

regard to strictly religious questions, but in business affairs, social relationships of all kinds, and political concerns as well.

Wesley's *Journal*, and the biographies of the early Methodist preachers, provide a large volume of evidence as to what efforts were made to enforce these Rules and Directions in the Bands, and evidence as to the state of discipline generally in the Societies. In January, 1741, Wesley met the Bands in Bristol and excluded about forty people, ' being determined that no disorderly walker should remain therein.' Moreover, he not only excluded people for active wrong, but also any one ' who was not known to and recommended by some on whose veracity I could depend.' [1] It was the same story in London the same year, and in both places the year following.[2] In March, 1743, at Newcastle, where the Society had numbered nearly 900, sixty-four were expelled on various grounds.[3] Nor, as the expulsion of Michael Fenwick, a preacher, in 1760, showed, did this discipline stop with the ordinary member. Even preachers of great popularity, men beloved by Wesley himself, were made to submit. Another striking case of discipline is reported in July, 1764 : ' I gave a fair hearing to two of our brethren who had proved bankrupts. Such we immediately exclude from our society, unless it plainly appears not to be their fault. Both these were in a prosperous way till they fell into that wretched trade of billbroking, wherein no man continues long without being wholly ruined . . . Yet it was quite clear that I— R— is an honest man : I would hope the same concerning the other.' [4] The disciplinary lash fell on a man who was admitted to be honest, but who had either been foolish or unfortunate. One of the questions dealt with at the annual Conferences was : ' What shall we do to prevent scandal, when any of our

[1] *Journal.* II, p. 429.   [2] *ibid,* II, pp. 440, 526.
[3] *ibid,* III, p. 71. Of these, two were expelled for cursing and swearing, two for habitual Sabbath-breaking, seventeen for drunkenness, two for retailing spirituous liquors, three for quarrelling and brawling, one for beating his wife, three for habitual, wilful lying, four for railing and evil-speaking, one for idleness and laziness, and twenty-nine for lightness and carelessness.
[4] *ibid,* V, p. 80. Writing to Thomas Wride on December 11, 1787— *Letters,* VIII, p. 26—Wesley said : ' It is no wonder that young man should be ruined who connected himself with that *execrable bill trade.* In London I expel every one out of our Society who had anything to do with it. Whoever endorses a bill (that is, promises to pay) for more than he is worth is either a fool or a knave.'

As the network of Methodist societies spread over the land, so in every place one could find a cohesive body of people living under the inspirations of the same beliefs and hopes, and guided, urged or restrained, by the same detailed rules and regulations. More than once, Wesley was told to his face that he could persuade people to do anything. We have seen one of the methods of persuasion he employed.

CHAPTER V

NONCONFORMITY AND THE STATE

No study of social and economic life can disregard the relevant political facts. The life of a people both affects and is affected by the attitude of the governing body; laws cannot for long run counter to popular sentiment and public opinion. The legal position of the Nonconformists, in the decade immediately after the Restoration, underwent a number of important changes. On April 4, 1660, Charles II issued the Declaration of Breda, in which occur these words: 'We do declare a liberty to tender consciences and that no man shall be disquieted or called in question, for Differences of Opinion in Matters of Religion which do not disturb the Peace of the Kingdom; and that we shall be ready to consent to such an act of Parliament, as, upon mature Deliberation, shall be offered to us, for the full granting that Indulgence.' This threw the onus on the House of Commons, which failed to agree on what constituted 'the true reformed Protestant religion.' On October 25, 1660, Charles, in a Declaration, renewed the sentiments expressed above. Then the following January saw Venner's Fifth Monarchy revolt, after which the King prohibited all unlawful and seditious meetings, and conventicles held under pretence of religious worship. Thereupon all sects were severely treated, the Quakers especially because of their refusal to take oaths.

In March, 1661, a mixed Commission of Episcopalians and Presbyterians, known as the Savoy Conference, attempted, without success, to find a plan of comprehension. In December of that year, Parliament passed the Corporation Act, under which all holding office in corporations, in which were many Dissenters, were to take an oath that they believed it unlawful to take up arms against the king. They were also to abjure the Solemn League and Covenant. In future, those elected to office were required to take the sacrament according to the rites of the Church of England.

The Act of Uniformity was passed in May, 1662, and came into operation on St. Bartholomew's Day, August 24. By this all ministers must declare their 'unfeigned assent and consent to all and everything contained and prescribed in and by the book intitled "The Book of Common Prayer."' In May of the next year, this Act was extended to include post-masters, as well as ministers and teachers, certificates of conformity being required. In December, 1662, Charles issued a declaration of indulgence to Catholic and Protestant Nonconformists and the February following attempted, unsuccessfully, to get Parliament to grant him power to dis-pense with the Act of Uniformity, although his declaration two months before had professed to do this.

The Conventicle Act of May, 1664, prohibited any meeting for Nonconformist worship of more than four persons, over and above members of a household. This Act affected the whole body of Nonconformists, whereas the Act of Uniformity had affected the ministers only. Yet the con-venticles went on secretly, except amongst the Quakers, who continued to hold their meetings publicly. The Five Mile Act, 1665, required all Nonconformist ministers to swear, *inter alia,* that they would not 'at any time endeavour any altera-tion of government either in Church or State.' If they declined the oath they were forbidden to come within five miles of any city, or corporate town, or borough. They were also forbidden to teach in schools.[1]

In August, 1667, Clarendon fell and the Cabal took his place. These penal laws then became almost dead letters and conventicles flourished more or less openly. The Conventicle Act lapsed in November, 1667. In July, 1669, Charles was persuaded to issue a Proclamation ordering Justices to execute the laws for the suppression of Conventicles, and especially to proceed against the preachers according to the Five Mile Act. The Second Conventicle Act was passed in May, 1670, and the next twelve months saw what was probably the worst persecution from which the Dissenters suffered. Then in March, 1672, was issued the Declaration

[1] The Five Mile Act, oppressive as it seems, may be regarded in another light. At this time it was known that certain of the dissenting preachers (such as Marsden, Gower, Hobson, Tillam, Wigan, Jones and Price—see *Baptist Historical Society Transactions,* Vol. I, No. 3, 1909, p. 151) were conspirators. Yet the Government required only that they should take an oath to be loyal to the *status quo,* the only penalty upon a refusal being as above stated.

of Indulgence, under which Protestant Nonconformists were allowed to worship publicly. From now the Nonconformists had comparative peace. In March, 1673, Parliament forced Charles to withdraw this Declaration, but the licences issued under it were not yet revoked. The Test Act of March, 1673, was aimed at the Papists, but fell also on Protestant Nonconformists who would not take the sacrament according to the Church of England rites. It made the sacrament the test for civil offices, which it remained until 1828.

In 1689 was passed the Toleration Act, which granted, with limitation, the right of religious worship to Protestant Nonconformists. Neither Unitarians nor Papists had relief by this Act, and from time to time measures against both were passed, but there was now a spirit of toleration abroad. The Tories, under Queen Anne, it is true, tried to revert to the methods of persecution, and in 1711 passed the Occasional Conformity Act. This punished with heavy fines any man who attended a Nonconformist chapel after having qualified for office by taking the sacrament. In 1714, the Schism Act aimed at circumventing the Toleration Act by forcing Dissenters' children to have an Anglican education. But the Queen died, and the advent to power of the Whigs under George I changed the situation, and in 1718 both these oppressive Acts were repealed. Freedom of worship was now achieved for the most part, but until the nineteenth century religious tests were maintained. This meant that a strict Nonconformist, one who would not take the Anglican sacrament, could neither hold office under the Crown nor in the Municipalities, and was excluded from the Universities.

The foregoing gives in brief outline the principal changes in the legal position of the Nonconformists, who were not, even so, altogether helpless in face of the persecution that periodically befell them.[1] The fact that Charles was opposed

---

[1] On January 13, 1671, J. Knightley, a Justice, wrote to Col. Samuel Sandys, M.P., complaining that 'Some conventicles . . . were convicted by me last October. One of them this sessions tried his appeal. But we were so careful, and had got so good a jury . . . a verdict (was) brought in for the king. But . . . the Court was hardly up before they arrested the informer with five several actions, the expense of which must necessarily undo a poor man—a rich one, indeed, is not able to wrestle with their united purse.' See C.S.P.D., 1671, p. 20. Even in 1671, there were ways and means of resisting oppression.

to persecution was in their favour, in so far as his attitude influenced the Justices in the application of the repressive laws. Nor were all the Bishops ill-disposed. Such men as Wilkins of Chester, and others of humanitarian feelings could not but pity the severity with which at certain times Nonconformists were treated.

In 1727, the Dissenters formed a useful association for political and other purposes. This consisted of Presbyterian, Congregational, and Baptist ministers who united under the general description of the ' Protestant Dissenting Ministers of the Three Denominations residing in and about the Cities of London and Westminster.' They addressed, as a body, the Throne on public occasions and resisted efforts to undo the policy of the Toleration Act, while their influence, amongst their own denominations, extended far beyond London itself. In 1732, a general meeting of Protestant Dissenters was held in Silver Street, London, with the object of considering an application for the repeal of the Corporation and Test Acts. Out of this, a body known as the ' Deputies,' representing the three Denominations within a radius of ten miles of London, grew, ' to protect the Civil Rights of the Protestant Dissenters.' [1] This is important as marking a definite stage in the struggle for religious and civil liberty, it being Nonconformity's first attempt at combination definitely for purpose of self-defence.[2] One of the great difficulties of the Dissenters, after the Toleration Act, lay in their liability to election to offices such as that of sheriff, which as we have seen, involved taking the sacrament in the Church. If they refused to do this, they could be, and often were, heavily fined. This gave an opportunity for the persecution of any particular Nonconformist by the simple means of electing him to office.[3]

[1] Anon: *A Sketch of the Deputies*, p. 1.   [2] Dale: *op. cit.*, p. 519.
[3] In 1754, Sheafe, Streatfield, and Evans, who were Dissenters, were fined £600 each for refusing to serve in London as sheriffs. Their fines, and those of others similarly, were expressly devoted towards the cost of building the new Mansion House. The case went to the Courts, where that against Streatfield broke down on a technicality, while Sheafe died before it was concluded. The issue was not decided until 1767, when Evans won his long fight, for Lord Mansfield, in the House of Lords, decided that a man could legally object to the validity of his election on the grounds that he had not taken the Sacrament (i.e. in the Church). This decision completely stopped that form of persecution. (A good account of this is given in Dale: *op. cit.*, p. 564.)

With this historical background of persecution, it is only to be expected that the Nonconformists would aim at religious liberty, even if they sometimes wanted a liberty they were unwilling should be given to others, such as the Roman Catholics. Desiring this liberty and working for it, it is not surprising that some became champions of civil liberty as well.

The next point to be considered is what philosophy of the State, if indeed any, was held by the Nonconformists. The Puritans had no one political philosophy. Some, as a section of the Anabaptists, had originally tended to a kind of anarchism which was capable of becoming acute in its opposition to the actual government, but in later times this anarchist attitude gave place to a simple indifference to politics. Others, such as the Levellers, were democrats, sometimes of an advanced sort. Yet others, amongst whom would be the bulk of the Presbyterians, were constitutionalists, representing perhaps the outlook of Calvin.

Baxter realized that there was a communistic side to Christianity, but this he did not consider to be of universal application. His intense sympathy with the oppressed rendered him, he knew, liable to a charge of being a Democrat, but the justice of such a charge he repudiated. Addressing the rich rack-renting landlords, he says: 'If easing your burdened, oppressed tenants seems so hard to you, what would you have said if he had tryed you as he did a rich man with a Goe and sell all that thou hast. . . . You think that this doctrine savours of the Levellers or Quakers. What would you have done if you had lived when the Spirit of love made all Christians sell all that they had and live in common?'[1] It was not moralists like himself, but grasping magnates such as they were, he urged, who evoked a spirit hostile to the customary order of things. 'There is no standing before the multitude if they be but armed with despair. . . . Interest ruleth the world. Use the people so well that they may feel that peace and obedience and the Kingdom's defence is their interest, and you take the most probable way of public safety.'[2]

The Dissenters generally were Hanoverian and supporters

[1] Baxter: *The Poor Husbandman's Advocate*, p. 48.
[2] *ibid*, p. 38.

the doors were defended by 3,000 or 4,000 people, who refused to move.'[1] He hoped the King would employ his Guards.

A climax was reached in London a few days later. On May 25, Richard Watts, writing to Williamson from Deal, said: 'His Royal Highness's going to London so suddenly gave rise to a false report that there was a rising in London; that the factious party had killed a great many people, and that the rebellion was increasing.'[2] On May 29, Sir John Robinson could write from the Tower to Williamson: 'Last night and this day's action have broken up all the large meetings in the City, and the King's late orders have very much encouraged us to proceed in it, so I dare be confident that peace will soon be restored.'[3] The authorities had been very alarmed and probably had exaggerated the situation, which none the less may have been of some seriousness. Although 1670-71 saw the height of the persecution of the Nonconformists, during the years that followed they were often suspect.[4] Their letters were continually intercepted, and a keen watch kept on their movements, which in the case of the more prominent were duly reported to London.

The fact of Nonconformity was itself a ground of suspicion. What could people be up to who by passive resistance disobeyed certain of the laws? Why should they have private meetings? Bunyan, in his own account of his imprisonment records his argument with a man named Cobb, who had been sent by the Justices to reason with him. Cobb attempted to put Bunyan in the wrong on grounds of religious principle. He argued: 'The King then commands you, that you should not have any private meetings; because it is against his law, and he is ordained of God, therefore you should not have any.' Bunyan replied: 'Paul did own the powers that were in his day, as to be of God; and yet he was often in prison under them for all that . . . The law hath provided two ways of obeying: the one to do that which I,

---

[1] C.S.P.D., pp. 233f.   [2] ibid, p. 236.   [3] ibid, pp. 239f.
[4] In 1683, for instance, we find search being made by the Deputy Lieutenants and others of the East Riding in the houses of Dissenters for arms, but they have to report to the Lord Lieutenant that they have found 'no considerable arms worth the naming.' Hist. MSS. Com., 3rd Report, p. 96.

in my conscience, do believe that I am bound to do, actively; and where I cannot obey actively there I am willing to lie down, and to suffer what they will do unto me.'[1] Many Nonconformists thought and acted in this way, but it was very unsatisfactory to those in authority.

Some of the Nonconformists, such as the Fifth Monarchists, were definitely disloyal, and no doubt others at times, but the usual attitude was one of loyalty to the actual monarch, and to the agents of the law, such as the Justices. This attitude was based on religious grounds, and however tortuous such a view as that expressed by Bunyan might seem to those who were in authority at the time, it was sincerely held by the generality of Nonconformists.

The religious ground of the normal loyalty of the Nonconformists, as of others who were not Nonconformists, is to be found in the thirteenth chapter of Romans, from which quotations were frequently made by leading preachers and writers. Nothing could be clearer than Baxter's statement of this when he preached before the House of Commons in the anxious days prior to the return of Charles II : 'As a papist must cease to be a papist if he will be truly and fully loyal to his sovereign . . . so a Protestant must so far cease to be a Protestant, before he can be disloyal. For Romans xiii. is part of the rule of his religion.'[2] In the *Christian Directory*, Baxter gave his 'Directions for Subjects concerning their duty to their Rulers.' He expressly denied that the fount of sovereignty was in the people. Basing his argument on Romans xiii. 1, he said : 'Rulers, therefore are God's officers, placed under Him in His kingdom . . . and they receive their power from God, who is the only original of power.'[3] In an involved argument as to the rightfulness of the Oath of Supremacy, Baxter pronounced in its favour on the grounds that it meant 'not that the king is chief in the spiritual government, by the keys of excommunication and absolution, but that he is chief in the coercive government about spiritual matters.' This did not mean that the power of the pastor was surrendered to the magi-

[1] *A Relation of the Imprisonment of Mr. John Bunyan*, pp. 232f.
[2] Baxter: *A Sermon of Repentance*, April 30, 1660, *Works*, XVII, p. 149.
[3] Baxter: *The Christian Directory*, *Works*, VI, pp. 23f.

strate, for the power of each was separate from the other.[1]

Views similar to those of Bunyan, himself a Baptist, appear in a Baptist Confession of Faith of 1660, which drew attention to another Scriptural passage. 'We believe that there ought to be civil Magistrates in all Nations, "for the punishment of evil doers, and for the praise of them that do well." 1 Peter ii. 14 . . . all men are obliged by Gospel rules, to be subject to the higher Powers. . . . But in case the Civil Powers . . . impose things about matters of Religion, which we through conscience to God cannot actually obey, then . . . we ought (in such cases) to obey God rather than men . . . humbly purposing (in the Lord's strength) patiently to suffer whatsoever shall be inflicted upon us.'[2] In another Baptist 'Confession,' of 1679, the forty-fifth article is entitled, 'Of the civil magistrate,' and lays it down that 'the office of a magistrate, may be accepted of, and executed by Christians, when lawfully called thereunto. . . . And subjection in the Lord ought to be yielded to the magistrates in all lawful things commanded by them, for conscience sake . . .'[3]

[1] Baxter: *The Christian Directory, Works,* VI, p. 55. 'An heretical preacher may be silenced by the king upon pain of banishment, and silenced by the church, upon pain of excommunication. . . . There is a magistrate's discipline, and a pastoral discipline. . . . To command upon pain of corporal punishment, that a heretic or impenitent, wicked man may forbear the sacred ordinances and privileges, a magistrate may do; but to command it only upon Divine and spiritual penalties, belongeth to the pastors of the church.' There is nothing of the democrat about Baxter; on the other hand his writings show him far from a royal sycophant.

[2] *Baptist Minutes,* I, p. 19.

[3] McGlothlin: *Baptist Confessions of Faith,* p. 158. These views of subjection to the civil power, based upon certain passages of Scripture, but limited by conscience, were commonly held by both Nonconformists and Anglicans at the time. Owing, however, to oppression, the question was of more practical import to the Nonconformists. Later, we find men in their ranks with other views. Priestley, in his *Essay on the First Principles of Government,* pp. 27f, said: 'Nothing can more justly excite the indignation of an honest and oppressed citizen, than to hear a prelate, who enjoys a considerable benefice, under a corrupt government, pleading for its support by those abominable perversions of Scripture . . . "the powers which be are ordained of God," and others of similar import. It is a sufficient answer to such an absurd quotation as this, that for the same reason, the powers which *will be* will be ordained of God also. . . . "All civil power is derived from God." . . . From this maxim it was a clear consequence, that the governments, which at any time subsist, being the ordinance of God, and the kings which are at any time upon the throne, being the vicegerents of God, must not be opposed.' See also, Price: *A Discourse on the love of our Country,* pp. 20-23, 'Obedience, therefore, to the laws and to magistrates, are necessary expressions of our regard to the community.'

The Quaker attitude towards the State and its organization is well known. Fox, writing to Cromwell, said: 'The magistrate is not to bear the sword in vain, who ought to be a terror to evil-doers; but as the magistrate that doth bear the sword in vain, is not a terror to evil-doers, so he is not a praise to them that do well.'[1] The function of the law and its administration was ethical, and this alone gave the right for one man to bear authority over another, seeing that fundamentally all men were equal. Quakers were expected not to take any part in the administration of the law, nor to exercise authority over others.[2] Just as they were to renounce worldly honours, they were not to accept official position; they were a people gathered and separated from the world. They did not regard the King in any way fundamentally different from other men. Like others, he should justify his existence by the conscientious discharge of his functions.[3] They did not seek to level men down, but held by implication a high doctrine of human personality, since every man might live in accordance with the dictates of a divine inner light. So in addressing King or magistrate, they would not employ a mode different from what they would use towards others, and this implied no disrespect, although it appeared so to others for a long while. They would not take an oath in a court of law or elsewhere, holding that the command, 'Let your yea be yea, and your nay, nay,'[4] was to be literally obeyed. In conflict with authority, the Quaker attitude was simple and consistent. Quakers continued to do openly what they believed to be right, and were quite prepared to endure the consequences. It was for the attitude of authority to change, not for them, seeing that in their actions they were guided by the Inner Light and by the plain teaching of the New Testament. Yet they were quite prepared to promise due obedience to the State, and to abstain from conspiracies. George Fox, replying to the charge of disloyalty brought

[1] *Journal of George Fox*, I, p. 246.
[2] Penn was criticized on this point at the beginning of his Pennsylvania experiment, see Graham: *William Penn*, p. 164.
[3] cf. Price: *op. cit.*, p. 23, 'Civil governors are properly the servants of the public; and a King is no more than the first servant of the public, created by it, maintained by it, and responsible to it. . . . His authority is the authority of the community.'
[4] Matthew v. 37, and James v. 12.

against Quakers, pointed out that their beliefs were such that
to resort to force was sin, and that their deliberate
attitude towards anything of which they did not approve was
to oppose it by their own suffering.[1] As the eighteenth
century wore on, the loyalty of the Dissenters came to be
taken for granted[2] but it was otherwise for a long while
in regard to the Methodists. Popular riots occurred because
this body was suspected of complicity in the designs of
France to assist the Stuart cause by a landing. Wesley and
his followers were suspected of being Papists, and doubt was
consequently felt as to their loyalty. This suspicion was
not unnatural. The Societies, composed chiefly of poor
people, meeting at unusual hours, admittance being often by
ticket, with their strict discipline, suggested the Jesuits, and
the fact that they were under the domination of one man
also suggested the Catholic religious orders. Why did the
Wesleys and their preachers constantly go up and down the
land, if not on some malevolent political scheme? We find
Wesley himself refraining from leaving London on a certain
day because on that day all Papists had been ordered to leave,
and he did not wish to risk giving apparent support to this
supposition of his connexion with them. While he was in
Cornwall, it was stated and believed by many that he had the
Young Pretender in disguise with him.

Wesley's own real loyalty to the Hanoverians was often
expressed in a way that seems fullsome and exaggerated, but
actually was quite sincere. A number of the Wesleys'
hymns were written for the King, the Prince of Wales,
Parliament, Magistrates.[3] They show he had no theory of

---

[1]Anon (George Fox): *The Remonstrance of the Suffering-People of
God, called Quakers,* pp. 14f. For a further refutation of disloyalty, see
Anon: *The Religious Assemblies of the People called Quakers
Vindicated.*

[2] A striking illustration of the loyalty of Dissenters to the Hanoverians
occurred in 1715 when James Wood, minister of a congregation at
Chowbent (Lancs.), 'headed a body composed of all the hale and
courageous men of his congregation, armed with the instruments of
husbandry, and marched them to Preston, and secured the possession of
Walton bridge, at the order of General Wills. George I acknowledged
this brave and loyal conduct. . . . Mr. Woods was after this, called
General Woods'—Toulmin: *An Historical view of the state of the
Protestant Dissenters,* p. 50.

[3] See Wesleys' Hymnals—Hymns and Sacred Poems, 1739, p. 18f;
Hymns for Times of Trouble, 1745, pp. 55f, 66f; Hymns of Intercession for All Mankind, 1758, pp. 11, 17f.

popular sovereignty, but regarded the King as functioning by Divine Right. He particularly regarded the Hanoverian monarchs as worthy of praise in that they stood in opposition to the Roman power, and also as representing the law were the means of holding in some check the violence of the mob so often directed against the Methodists. In 1744, Wesley drew up an address, on behalf of the Methodist Societies, which he proposed giving to the King.[1] In this he promised full obedience 'consistent with the written Word of God.'[2] The implication is that in a conflict between the commands of the King and the teaching of the Bible, the latter must prevail, and in matters of interpretation of the Bible the enlightened individual conscience is the final arbiter. In the long run, it was not the King, but the conscience that was supreme, nevertheless the King is not lightly to be disobeyed.[3] As Wesley was for the Methodists largely the standard of interpretation of the Bible, not only because of his general influence and his preaching, but through his *Notes on the New Testament*,[4] so in practice he exercised a considerable influence in directing the Methodist attitude towards the King and Government. His letters contain abundant evidence, similarly, as to his views concerning loyalty to the King and Magistracy. Nor does he stop with preaching loyalty. We find him in 1775 writing to the Earl of Dartmouth, Secretary of State for the Colonies, to give warning that there were large numbers of disaffected men in the country.[5] He explained the reasons—serious decay of trade, dearness of food, pressure of unemployment. Some two months later he again wrote to Dartmouth, asserting that the people were out for the King's blood. In a private letter of 1789, he said, 'I suppose everyone that loves King George loves Mr. Pitt.'[6] Wesley's loyalty to the throne included a loyalty to the King's Ministers, even when he did not agree with them, and to Parliament. The Methodist attitude was officially defined thus, 'What directions shall be given concerning our conduct to the civil Government? None of us shall, either in writing or conversation, speak lightly or irreverently of the Govern-

---

[1] He was dissuaded by his brother, however, from presenting it, on the grounds that such action would constitute Methodism a separate sect.
[2] *Journal*, III, pp. 123f.   [3] cf. the attitude of Bunyan.
[4] Published in 1755.   [5] *Letters*, VI, pp. 158f.   [6] *ibid*, VIII, p. 113.

ment under which he lives.'[1] Writing in 1782, in reply to
criticisms he had heard, Wesley dealt with the questions as to
whether a Christian minister ought to preach politics. His
view was that politics in the narrower sense ought not to
come within the province of the minister as such, but if a
minister heard in any place slanders uttered against the King
or his Ministers, it was his bounden duty to be out-
spoken.[2]

We pass from the political integrity of Nonconformists to
their political importance, from the expression of their loyalty
to the use of their votes. Here the unpublished Evans' MS.
(1715), from which we have already drawn largely in our
numerical discussion, can supply certain interesting details
which indicate the considerable political strength of contemporary Dissent, although its returns are certainly incomplete. The totals recorded show 14,646 County and Borough
voters in England (including Monmouth) and 2,021 voters
for magistrates. The corresponding figures for Wales are
603 and 115 respectively.[3] From this MS. we learn that at
Whitehaven, Cumberland, the ' Dissenters here by Trade have
such an influence at Cockermouth, that with the Dissenters of
Cockermouth, they return as they please.' A somewhat
similar story is related in regard to the South-west, for in
Devonshire, we are told, ' the influence of Trading Dissenters
very extensive over their Dependents in Business.' And, ' the
Burrough (sic) Towns, where his Majesty has any friend
chosen, have that interest chiefly supported by the Dissenters,
as at Plymouth, Plympton, Tavistock, Ashburton, Honiton,
Tiverton, &c. . . . In the county they are supposed to be
about one-sixth of the freeholders.' Going over the border
into Somerset, we find at Minehead that ' Dissenters can

---

[1] *Methodist Minutes* (1862 edit.), p. 270.
[2] *Works*, XI, p. 148. Bradburn, who was President of the Wesleyan
Conference in 1799, published a sermon to show that unlimited religious
liberty was consistent with a steadfast attachment to King and
Constitution. He was opposing some of the ideas of Parliamentary
reform then advocated—see Blanshard : *The Life of Samuel Bradburn,*
p. 143.
[3] See Appendix VII. The interest which this MS. reveals in the
Dissenters' voting strength may be understood, for in 1710 following the
Sacheverell case, the Whig Ministry of Godolphin had given way to a
Tory Government under St. John and Harley, and a renewed persecution
of Nonconformists was threatened—the Schism Act, 1714, dates from
about the time this MS. was being compiled.

influence in this Borough at Elections thirty besides the seventy-five Dissenters who are voters themselves.' Concerning Bristol, it is stated that the Dissenting voting power for the city is 700 or upwards, while there are seventy-two or more voters for Gloucestershire, and fifty or upwards for Somersetshire, who also reside in Bristol. In fact, ' the strength of all the Dissenters (i.e. including Quakers) may justly be reckoned much more than that of all the Low Church Party there.' Regarding the Bristol voters, the MS. adds that they ' by their estates and interest in Trade, can make many 100 more votes (upon an election) in Bristol, Gloucestershire, Somersetshire, Monmouthshire, Herefordshire, Wales; and the cities of Gloucester and Hereford; the town of Monmouth, &c.' In reference to the voting strength for Gloucestershire, the writer complacently adds, ' Low Church can hardly make up thirty,' while in respect of Somersetshire, he informs us, ' Low Church not near the number.' [1] The data of this sort in the MS. emphasizes the solid nature of the political support which the Dissenters were able to rally, at a critical time, to the support of the incoming Hanoverians.

We find Wesley concerned with the ethical aspect of voting at elections. His *Journal* often shows on the same page a blending of religious matters, humanitarian projects, and political concerns. In 1751, he journeyed to Oxford especially to vote.[2] In 1747, at St. Ives, Cornwall, he ' spoke severally to those who had votes in the ensuing election. I found them such as I desired. Not one would even eat or drink at the expense of him for whom he voted. Five guineas had been given to W.C., but he returned them immediately. T.M. positively refused to accept anything; and when he heard that his mother had received money privately he could not rest until she give him the three guineas, which he instantly sent back.' [3]

In his ' Word to a Freeholder,' Wesley dealt with this common practice of bribery. He reminded the voter that his oath required him to swear that he had not received ' gift or reward, directly or indirectly, nor any promise of any, on

[1] The Thompson MS. (1773) unfortunately gives no information of this sort.
[2] *W.H.S.*, XV, p. 134.
[3] *Journal*, III, p. 305.

account of your vote.' Therefore, 'I hope you have received
nothing else, neither will receive; no entertainment, no meat
or drink. If this is given on account of your vote you are
perjured still.'[1] He urged men to vote for candidates who
were God-fearing and loyal to the King.[2] He commanded his
preachers to second his efforts to extirpate bribery at
elections.[3] In 1774, Wesley was in Bristol at election time,
when the American War was about to begin. He advised the
voters of the Society to vote conscientiously and to avoid
railing at those who voted the other way.[4]

We now come to a brief consideration of the attitude of
the Nonconformists towards the American and French
Revolutions. Nonconformists could not stand aside, un-
interested, when the conflict with America developed, yet they
were not unanimously in support of either side. Amongst
them two eminent men may be cited as evidence of this
division of opinion—Dr. Richard Price and Wesley. Price
wrote one of the most important treatises on the American
War, entitled, 'Observations on the Nature of Civil Liberty,
the Principles of Government, and the Justice and Policy of
the War with America.' This was published in 1776, when
60,000 copies were sold. The City of London gave him its
thanks and freedom for it, and it exercised considerable
influence upon public opinion.[5] In 1778, Congress conferred
American citizenship on Price and asked his assistance in the
organization of its finances. Price followed the Locke
tradition, with modifications. Liberty, he argued, implied self-
government, from which it followed that every man was his
own legislator. Therefore, taxes are but 'free gifts for
public services.' Parliamentary sovereignty is incompatible
with real self-government. Liberty is inalienable, and if it

[1] *Works*, XI, p. 187. This pamphlet was first published in 1748; again in
1767 and 1783.
[2] *ibid*, XI, p. 188.
[3] *ibid*, VIII, pp. 296f.
[4] *W.H.S.*, XV, p. 135. The Quakers also had something to say concerning the 'corrupt and immoral practices which have frequently
attended public elections.' The 'drunkenness, riot and confusion' of these
occasions not only called for personal care on the part of the Quaker;
he ought also to use his influence to the contrary—Society of Friends:
The Book of Christian Discipline, p. 132.
[5] Thomas: *Richard Price*, p. 74. In 1777, Price wrote a supplement to
this work, entitled, *Additional Observations*.

be lost, then the people 'must have a right to emancipate themselves as soon as they can.' [1]

Wesley's attitude towards the Americans underwent some modification as time passed. In the summer of 1775, he wrote to the Earl of Dartmouth : ' All my prejudices are against the Americans. For I am . . . bred up from my childhood in the highest notions of passive obedience and non-resistance. And yet, in spite of all my rooted prejudices, I cannot avoid thinking . . . that an oppressed people asked for nothing more than their legal rights . . .' [2] In the same year, Wesley published his ' Calm Address to our American Colonies.' In this he argued that the English Parliament had the right to tax the Americans because an English Colony was simply a number of persons to whom the King had granted a Charter. If it were replied that the Americans ought not to be taxed seeing they had no representation in Parliament, then the same argument implied that the English Parliament had no right to make any laws affecting the Americans, which, said Wesley, was a right no one had queried. If they had a right to English privileges they were accountable to English laws. He pointed out that the Americans were descended from men who either had no votes or else resigned them by emigration, therefore it was useless for them to argue that they possessed all the privileges of their ancestors. He further urged that a few years before, when the Americans were in need, the Mother Country sent help, and now reasonably desired to be re-imbursed for the expense, and to that end had ' laid a small tax (which she always had a right to do) on one of her colonies.' [3] He admitted that this small tax could hardly be the cause of so much trouble, and gave it as his opinion that the real cause of the conflict was to be found in the inflammatory work of those in England, who, said Wesley, hate monarchy and hope by trouble in America to overturn the government in England, and establish a new order.

On November 29 of the same year, 1775, Wesley wrote to *Lloyd's Evening Post* defending himself against calumniation on his writing the ' Calm Address.' He said that having opportunity more than any living man of observing the state

---

[1] Price : *Observations on the Nature of Civil Liberty*, pp. 3, 6, 15, 50.
[2] *Letters*, VI, p. 156.   [3] *Works*, XI, p. 82.

of affairs in the country, he was aware of how many men were deliberately trying to make trouble by saying : ' How unjustly, how cruelly, the King is using the poor Americans, who are only contending for their liberty and for their legal privileges ! ' [1]   So, he argued, the only way was to show that the Americans were not wrongly treated. ' With this view, to quench the fire, by laying the blame where it was due, the Calm Address was written.' [2]   A month later, in a private letter to Christopher Hopper, Wesley, after repeating his general position, added, ' But I say, as Dean Tucker, " Let them drop." Cut off all other connexion with them than we have with Holland or Germany. Four-and-thirty millions they have cost us to support them since Queen Anne died. Let them cost us no more. Let them have their desire and support themselves.' [3]

Early in the next year, 1776, Wesley published ' A Seasonable Address to the More Serious Part of the Inhabitants of Gt. Britain.' This was an appeal on religious grounds so to act as to bring about peace : ' Let everyone remember his own sin, and not his neighbour's.' [4]   In the same year, he published a pamphlet entitled, ' The Unhappy Contest between us and our American Brethren,' in which he condemned the folly and sin of deciding international questions by war. ' A Calm Address to the Inhabitants of England,' [5] was published in 1777, and was at once a sequel to the ' Calm Address to our American Colonies ' of two years earlier, and also a reply to the ' Observations ' of Dr. Price. Wesley claimed that 50,000 to 100,000 copies of this were dispersed, in newspapers and otherwise, throughout Great Britain and Ireland. The argument was that since the National Fast proclaimed by the King, England had got back to God, and that as a consequence, the tide of struggle had turned. England was surely going to win, and Wesley appealed to all for loyalty to Throne and Government.

The importance of Wesley in influencing public opinion on American questions lay not only in his personal influence with a large body of people, and the enormous circulation of his writings, but also in the fact that by this time Methodism had

---

[1] *Letters,* VI, p. 193.   [2] *ibid,* VI, p. 199.
[3] *Works,* XI, p. 122.   [4] *ibid,* XI, p. 199.   [5] *ibid,* XI, pp. 123ff.

already taken firm hold in America.[1] He was a man, therefore, with strong personal interests, and a large personal
following on both sides of the Atlantic. His theories might
sometimes be wide of the mark; his facts were usually correct
and obtained in advance of the knowledge of most others.
We find him in 1775, before the home government had realized
the seriousness of the struggle from the military point of view,
warning Lord North, the Prime Minister, that he knew from
information supplied by his own preachers in America, that
the Colonists were not merely peaceful farmers 'ready to run
at the sight of a red-coat,' but a well-trained and well-
disciplined body of volunteers, 'terribly united.'

The large majority of those Englishmen who sympathized
with the French Revolution were Nonconformists, amongst
whom the Unitarians were remarkable for the unanimity with
which they welcomed the upheaval in 1789. Drs. Price and
Priestley were in the van, the latter in opposition to Burke.
Gilbert Wakefield, another Unitarian, took the place vacant
by the departure later of Priestley for America, but warned
both sides that violence could do little or no good. Robert
Hall, the leading Baptist of the day, declared that the Revolution was 'the most splendid event in history.'[2] Baptists, and
others, however, might regard the Revolution on the other
side of the Channel as glorious, without being in the least
prepared to see it repeated on this. In 1798, the Rev. John
Martin, a minister of that persuasion, said in a sermon that
'should the French land, some, yea, many, of these . . .
(Dissenters) would unite to encourage the French.' The
result of this sermon was the rapid expulsion of the preacher,
who succeeded in arousing the anger of almost the entire
Denomination.[3] William Godwin, the author of the *Enquiry
Concerning Political Justice,* and a keen sympathiser with
the French Revolution, was the son of a Dissenting minister,

[1] In 1776, the year of the signing of the Declaration of Independence,
there were 4,921 members in America. The American Methodist body
was suspected of being an organization of Tory propaganda. Like all
other communities at the time, it was not unanimous in political sentiment and allegiance. Asbury, the great leader of American Methodism,
writing to Rankin (one of the preachers in England) stated his affection
for America to be too great to permit him to leave it, and that he
believed the Americans would win in the struggle—*N.H.M.,* II, p. 81.

[2] *The Cambridge Modern History,* VIII, p. 764.

[3] Halévy: *A History of the English People in* 1815, Book III, p. 373.

had been educated at the Hoxton Academy under Dr. Kippis, and was for a while in charge of a congregation himself. By this time, Godwin had ceased to be a minister, and later asserted that he was an atheist at the time when he was producing his book, returning to a vague theism later owing to the influence of Coleridge.[1] Although not an original reformer himself, his writings were hailed with delight by the younger among the feverishly enthusiastic would-be reformers.[2] The Methodists, unlike many of their fellow Nonconformists, did not join in any advocacy of revolutionary principles.

---

[1] *D.N.B.*, art. William Godwin.
[2] Beer: *History of British Socialism*, I, p. 114.

CHAPTER VI

THE DOCTRINE OF PERSONAL RESPONSIBILITY

WHENEVER the Christian religion is taken seriously it produces, in a greater or lesser degree, a sense of the personal responsibility of the individual to God for the right use of his possessions, of which he then regards himself as only the steward. In its most complete form this attitude is a way of life, for if a man regards himself and his possessions as a solemn trust from God, his whole conduct must be thereby modified, and we find this drastic view of stewardship coming to the fore from time to time in Christian history. At other times, it is limited, at least in practice, to particular aspects of life, while there are always special matters in regard to which its immediate relevance is noticeably felt. It may stress either the obligation of charity, the repression of luxury, the importance of vocation, the proper use of one's time, the responsibility of right expenditure, the disposal of one's wealth, or any two or more of these. Further, this doctrine always has social repercussions chiefly through its teaching on economic matters. Catholic and Anglican, as well as Nonconformist writers, have at times laid stress on it, but the doctrine of personal responsibility is likely to come more to the fore in Protestant Churches of the type of English Nonconformity since they make no claim to infallibility on the one hand, or to a State connexion on the other, and consequently tend to place more responsibility on the individual. In fact it may be said that the doctrine of stewardship is fundamental to the Nonconformist outlook.

This doctrine may be regarded as a middle position between communism and extreme individualism. In the Anabaptist and Digger movements we see the communist trend active, while Independency inclined the other way. Within the compass of the New Testament we have the communism of the infant Church at Jerusalem, the lively individualism of St.

Paul, and clear statements of the doctrine of stewardship.[1] Within our period, the statement of what is understood as stewardship sometimes varies a little, but the differences are not as a rule very marked. What is more noticeable is the motive underlying the insistence on this doctrine. Sometimes the motive is predominently the need of others, an appeal to the charitable sentiment based on the theological dogma of the sole ownership of everything by God. At other times the motive is a self-regarding one, namely, to seek to ensure one's own eternal happiness by the practice of stewardship in this life. Often these motives are mixed, and to them is added a socially expedient view that the practice of stewardship would lead to the well-being of the Commonwealth. This doctrine had been prominent in the period preceding the Restoration, and for it, however imperfectly, the Puritan view of life stood. The emphasis which the Puritan placed upon the Bible, which is saturated with this idea in both the Old and New Testaments, encouraged the stewardship view of life. The Commonwealth at its best was an attempt to govern the country on the basis of a solemn trust from God, however imperfectly the attempt may have succeeded, and however disingenuously some Parliamentarians and others may have acted. With the Restoration, a wave of reaction against over-strictness caused many in Court circles, and perhaps in others, to live in an irresponsible and unrestrained fashion contrary to that view of life which was based upon this doctrine. The resulting conflict of views is revealed by the sanctions with which divines, both Anglican and Dissenting, tried to keep alive the idea of stewardship in relation to what has always been its principal object—money or wealth. They preached almsgiving as the natural outcome of a stewardship of money on the ground that it paid in material ways. The very title of a work by the Dissenter, Thomas Gouge, is significant, *Riches Increased by Giving to the Poor*.[2] Gouge admitted that a man might become poor through his lack of business aptitude, but asserted 'that a penuriousness towards the Poor is the readiest way to

[1] cf. Acts iv. 32-37, vi. 1-6; 2 Cor. viii. 13-15, ix. 5-13; Matt. xxv. 14-30, xxiv. 45-51.

[2] It had recommendatory prefaces by other leading Dissenters, viz. Drs. Owen, Manion, and Bates, and Mr. Baxter.

poverty : so Christian Charity, rightly performed, is the surest
way to plenty and abundance, it being usually rewarded with
temporal benefits here, as well as with eternity hereafter.'[1]
In the period following a religious revival there is always a
tendency to fall back upon the prudential argument.

In the last year of the seventeenth century, Bellers had
advanced a view of stewardship which was specially related
to the leisured classes. He felt that stewardship must go
deeper than mere charity. 'And so much as men by the
greatness of their estates are excused from labour to earn
their bread, so much are they the greater stewards by their
leisure, opportunity and interest, to direct the Poor in their
labour, and to influence and instruct them to virtue (and not
to give away their estates to them).'[2] Baxter, similarly, urged
that the rich had different responsibilities from those of the
poor. 'It is not the toilsome drudgery of the vulgar which
we take to be all rich folk's duty; but idleness and
unprofitableness is a sin in the richest. Any of them may find
good work enough that is fit for them if they be willing.
Children, and servants, and friends, and neighbours, and
tenants, have souls and bodies which need their help. None
can say, "God found us no work to do," or that God gave
them more time or wealth than they had profitable use for.'[3]

The last and in some ways the most serious, act involving
the practice of this stewardship, concerns the disposal of one's
estate, a point considered by the Quakers, and by both Baxter
and Wesley. Friends were advised in 1691 by their London
Yearly Meeting, and at subsequent times, not to delay making
their wills and were assured that ' making wills in due time
can shorten no man's days.' In 1782, Friends were told
to ' have a strict regard to justice and equity and not be
actuated by caprice and prejudice, to the injury of those who
may have a reasonable expectation from their kindred or near
connexion . . . (and were warned) against undue care as to
the future. . . . Even where arrangements may be legally
secure, it is very questionable how far it is, in ordinary cases,
consistent with a sound and enlightened judgement, to attempt,

---

[1] Gouge : *Riches Increased by Giving to the Poor*, p. 11.
[2] Bellers : *Essays about the Poor, Manufactures* . . . p. 15.
[3] Baxter : *How to do good to many*, *Works* XVII, p. 302.

by our short-sighted posthumous provisions, to anticipate the
wants or responsibilities of those who must succeed us.'[1]
Baxter argued that a man should not leave his estate, however near the relationship, to any one whom the testator considered likely to mismanage it, to use it as a means of
forwarding a wicked life, or by it to live idly. Instead, the
estate should be left to ' some that are more likely to do good
with it, and to use it for God, and the public benefit.'[2] Wesley
warned parents not to leave money to a child if they had
reason to fear that particular child would prove wasteful. ' If
I had one child, elder or younger, who knew the value of
money, one who I believed would put it to the true use, I
should think it my absolute, indispensable duty to leave that
child the bulk of my fortune; and to the rest just as much
as would enable them to live in the manner they had been
accustomed to do.'[3] Characteristically, Wesley put his
injunction in a positive form—money must be left to the
one best able to look after it.

The Methodist argued that if each human being is strictly
accountable for everything in his life to God, it must follow
that should he act as a faithful steward, God would deal
accordingly with him. Therefore, a fully converted man
might be expected to prosper in his calling. This, however,
did not mean that his prosperity was a reward from God for
his faithfulness, which would give a wholly wrong importance
to success. On the contrary, a man has this success because
he has proved his ability to receive a greater stewardship.[4]
Hence, normally, failure in business, so far from meriting
pity, was deserving of blame, yet business success did not
necessarily follow a faithful stewardship. Equally important
for success in business was long and hard work, which was
demanded both by considerations of Christian ethics and
economics.

This doctrine of stewardship, or personal responsibility,
became of great importance in Methodism because it linked
together the salvation of the soul and worldly success, interests
apparently incompatible. It was true that the former might

[1] Society of Friends : *The Book of Christian Discipline*, pp. 124f.
[2] Baxter : *How to do good to Many, Works*, XVII, p. 326.
[3] *Sermons*, II, p. 323.
[4] cf. Parable of the Talents.

be achieved without the latter, but the getting of riches became something that the Christian pilgrim on his way to Heaven could take in his stride. A very real problem arose as to what to do with riches once they were obtained. To this a simple solution was offered: they could and should be given away. The same conclusion had been reached and taught in the Middle Ages, but whereas almsgiving was then enjoined as a means of acquiring merit, it was regarded by the Methodists rather as a consequence of a saving faith already possessed.[1] Wesley's views in this connexion, although they received more elaboration and articulation after his evangelical conversion in 1738, originated earlier. It is probable that he imbibed them germinally from his mother, while it is certain that both at Oxford and in Georgia, he practised a rigorous stewardship himself.[2]

Personal responsibility involved more than a stewardship of money. In particular it involved a right use of time. We have already seen that both Baxter and Bellers felt this strongly in regard to the leisured classes. It applied, however, to all. The Methodist attitude received formal expression: 'What ought we to avoid next to luxury? Idleness: or it will destroy the whole work of God on the soul.'[3] From his Oxford days, Wesley had practised a rigorous discipline in his use of time, not, as might be supposed, easily.[4] He deliberately linked time and money in one stewardship. He regarded it as impossible that a man in business should have any spare time.[5] If such a man had finished what he had in hand at a particular moment, and had nothing immediately requiring attention, then he should be thinking out how to improve his methods of business. A proper use of time will prevent business falling into a rut. Hence a proper steward-

---

[1] This view is present in a sermon analysed on pp. 116ff.

[2] *Preachers*, I, p. 156—shews that Wesley's preachers adopted his standpoint. and sometimes his manner.

[3] *Minutes* (1862 edit.), p. 716, Rowell's notes of the 1752 Conference. Idleness had, of course, long been regarded by the Church as wrong and dangerous; it was one of the Seven Deadly Sins.

[4] He makes it clear that he found it very difficult to use his time sacrificially. He liked to be idle often, to waste time, as he would regard it, on novel-reading, and on various recreations, including dancing. But every moment as well as every shilling, must be accounted for. Hence his diaries record how he spent each quarter hour of the day.

[5] Defoe similarly, see *infra*, p. 113.

business prosperity of many, due to hard application and to the direction of a large part of the profits into the business again, profits which might have been spent on pleasure if such expenditure had not been frowned upon. A third result was an alliance between religion and economic activity, closer than would otherwise have been the case. This last implied a measure of discipline by the Church of the business concerns of its members, the degree of which, as we have seen, varied as between the denominations, and from one period to another.

This view of one's calling implied an approximation of work and worship, both theologically and psychologically. Theologically, because from the days of the Garden of Eden and the Fall, God had ordained that man should live by the sweat of his brow; therefore labour owed its institution to a Divine decree. Man, being the steward of God must work for the glory of God, in such work and in such a way as God would approve. Merely to get wealth and to give it away is not enough. 'For vain and earthly designs are no more allowable in our employments, than in our alms and devotions. . . . But as our alms and devotions are not acceptable service but when they proceed from a pure intention, so our common employment cannot be reckoned a service to Him but when it is performed with the same piety of heart.'[1] Work and worship are not to be regarded as mutually exclusive—*Laborare est orare*. For every man there is a right calling, a right way of working in that calling, and a right purpose for which the calling should be prosecuted. Baxter dealt with the question as to whether work ought, or might be allowed, to interfere with worship. 'Must not all business give place to secret prayer? No. There are businesses of greater obligation which must be preferred. . . . A physician, in case of necessity, may omit all prayer, to go help to save a sick man's life. . . . And poor men that cannot spend time from their labour, are not bound to spend as much time in reading and prayer as rich men. . . .'[2] Defoe, in *The Complete English Tradesman*, similarly pointed out that acts of piety are not always to have precedence over acts of

---

[1] *Sermons*, II, pp. 317f.
[2] Baxter: *The Poor Man's Family Book, Works*, XIX, p. 503.

business, and uses the illustration of a husband who went for a midwife and stayed in the way to hear a sermon. Wesley, in writing to Arthur Keene, who had been steward of the Dublin Society for more than thirty years, urged him to 'be diligent in business, as one branch of the business of life.' [1] The business of life is the salvation of the soul which involves God's service in perfect obedience to His will, and of this industrial and commercial concerns are a part.

This congruence of worship and work has also a psychological aspect. Samuel Bradburn, one of the best known of Wesley's helpers, speaking of his earlier experiences, as an employee, said: 'Two things I have often observed, in which many people are wrong: first, supposing that attending to religion will make a man negligent in his business; and secondly, that being diligent in business has a tendency to make him careless about religion. I have frequently proved the very reverse of these reasonings, never finding a greater inclination to work than when my soul was happy in God. Nor did I ever feel much greater happiness, than sometimes when busy at work.' [2] William Crister, of Tyneside, felt much the same. 'People talk about not being able to get through their work. There is nothing like the love of God for this. I can get through twice as much with it, as without it. It bears the mind with cheerfulness above it, and inspires the body with fresh energy to do it.' [3] Such was the ordinary experience of men who knew nothing about psychological analysis, but who found as a fact that they could praise God in the workshop and work more efficiently as they did so, even as they would in the chapel 'engage' or 'labour' in prayer—significant words.

Amongst these Nonconformists who, in a greater or lesser degree, held this doctrine of personal responsibility, was very often found an attitude of mind described somewhat vaguely as 'otherworldliness.' It is true that people might be otherworldly to a degree, and irresponsible in respect of their possessions, their time, and their opportunities. Nevertheless, an acceptance of the principle of stewardship

[1] *Letters*, VI, p. 317.
[2] Blanshard: *The Life of Samuel Bradburn*, p. 19.
[3] Everett: *The Walls-end Miner*, p. 51.

is apt to be accompanied by an otherworldly outlook. Similarly, mystics, contrary to the supposition of many, are often highly practical people. The term 'otherworldly,' it should be noted, is used to cover two distinct views. According to the one, this life and all that belongs to it is evil, or at best, worthless, in which case religion is incompatible with a concern for social change. According to the other, the supreme importance of the future life is such that this life is either relatively unimportant, or important only as a preparatory experience. It is true that the language of Puritanism often, and its practice sometimes, appears at first sight to lend colour to the former of these conceptions. Baxter's belief in the need of frequent funeral sermons, for example,[1] and the statement of the celebrated Wesleyan preacher, John Nelson, that he had 'no business in this world but to get well out of it,'[2] seem to imply a complete contempt for this life. Yet we find that for all his insistence on life as a 'continual preparation for death,' Baxter was deeply concerned for the hard lot of the poor rack-rented husbandman, while there are many instances which show that Puritans of successive generations could be no less practical than pious. Such men were otherworldly in the sense that they believed in the immeasurable importance of the life hereafter and in the reality of the judgement-bar of Christ before which all must appear; but that did not necessarily rob this life of importance for them. They were not indifferent to this world, but saw it constantly in its relation to the next. The Puritan aimed at being a saint, the root idea of which term is one of separation. He sought to avoid being of the world, but he was in it none the less, for good or evil. If he were ascetic, it was rather because he felt the danger to the soul of indulgence than because he despised those things of this world which he might otherwise

---

[1] Baxter: *The Poor Man's Family Book, Works,* XIX, p. 539, 'Some would have no funeral sermons, and I would have almost no other. All our religion is but a continual preparation for death; to learn to die well, by learning, and practising to believe, and love, and live well.'

[2] *Preachers,* I, p. 132, 'I want neither (the world's) riches nor honours, but the honour that cometh from God only; I regard neither its smiles nor its frowns; and have no business in it but to get well out of it.' To get *well* out of the world did not mean that it could be ignored; rather the contrary.

have enjoyed.[1] Puritans equated life in all its manifold variety and commonplace detail with religion, and this identification lies at the base of their social influence. The concern of modern England with social questions follows the Puritan Revolution; it did not precede it, although there were individuals with socially awakened consciences before. And it was the Nonconformists who were the chief heirs of the Puritan tradition.

The Quakers are justly famous for their social views and work, yet they were otherworldly in the sense just described. It is true that they tended to develop a segregated life,[2] partly due to persecution and partly due to a fear of lapsing into ' worldliness,' but not due to any feeling of the worthlessness of this life.

The Methodist movement, the principal eighteenth-century representation of the Puritan spirit, is stated by J. L. and B. Hammond to have been a ' call not for citizens, but for saints.' [3] As to the prime object of the Revival this is true, but it needs qualification as regards the effects. In face of criticism, Wesley was able to appeal to the fact that, in one area and another, not only had individuals been ' saved,' but social life transformed. He, and some of his followers, attacked social abuses, tried schemes of social amelioration, and displayed an intense interest in the welfare of the country. As men who were in the world they were citizens; as men who were not of it, they were saints. Furthermore, sainthood has as one of its by-products, good citizenship. The interests of this life were not ignored, but dominated by the passionate interest displayed in the future. This led to an undue emphasis being placed upon death. The urgent attendance of Methodists upon the condemned criminal in

[1] cf. Baxter : *The Poor Husbandman's Advocate*, p. 47, ' I am not calling you all into Monastries or Hermitages. But hath God and His service been your *chiefe* delight? '

[2] Quakers strongly discouraged mixed marriages or anything in the nature of a worldly approach to marriage. The Yearly Meeting of 1722 sent out an Epistle which said : ' Parents are tenderly advised not to make it their first or chief care to obtain for their children large portions; but rather to be careful that their children be joined in marriage with persons of religious inclinations, suitable dispositions and temper, sobriety in manners, and diligence in business; and carefully to guard against all mixed marriages.'—Society of Friends : *Book of Christian Discipline*, p. 78.

[3] Hammond : *The Town Labourer*, p. 282.

order to save his soul, it might be upon the very scaffold, combined with the importance which their biographies show them to have placed upon the last hours of a person's life, indicate the depth of their belief that an individual's eternal welfare might be determined by a changed attitude of mind and heart, occurring even at the last moment. This must not blind us, however, to the fact that it was the business of everyone converted in the Revival to see that he so lived as to be able to face fearlessly the Judgement Day, and this amongst other things involved good citizenship, seeing that the whole life of each person would then be passed in review.

'Otherworldliness' and 'resignation' are often associated with one another. The 'resignation' of the Methodist was a real thing, but it was a resignation of worldly desire, and not in fact a resignation to worldly conditions; it was a resignation to the will of God rather than to the will of man.[1] In point of fact, the eighteenth century found these people, poor and uncultured for the most part, extremely obstinate, both in the Army and civil life. They had a way often of moulding their environment to suit their convictions, rather than of submitting. Men, otherworldly and resigned in the way described, have a habit of being uncompromising and often passionate moral reformers because of their desire to abolish sin, and so in effect become social reformers, since sin abolished implies injustice removed. Further, we find them directly attacking various forms of injustice without laying exclusive emphasis on the aspect of sin. Thus did a view of the relationship of man and his Maker which emphasized the direct personal responsibility to God of the individual in every sphere of human activity, become a powerful force in social life. When a man's relation towards God is one both of dependence and responsibility, his concern for his fellows is bound to be deepened since he can no longer do what he likes with his own—indeed he has nothing he can strictly call his own. So individual stewardship leads to social readjustment.

---

[1] *Sermons*, II, p. 224, 'By repentance and lowliness of heart the deadly disease of pride is healed; that of self-will by resignation, a meek and thankful submission to the will of God; and for the love of the world in all its branches, the love of God is the sovereign remedy.'

charity must both be taken into account. If possible, the
man to whom the would-be seller offered his goods should
loan money to prevent the necessity of selling at a sacrifice.
If unable to do this, he should try to get someone else to
make the loan.[1] *The Christian Directory* dealt also with the
ethical issue involved when the value of goods is found afterwards to have been considerably greater than the price actually
paid, as sometimes in the case of jewels. The buyer was
directed to give the seller an additional sum if the latter had
agreed to the bargain in genuine and reasonable ignorance of
the true value. But if the trader ought to have known the
proper value, as when a man is selling goods which it was
his ordinary trade to sell, then his inefficiency might be
penalized and no additional money pass over.[2]

The above cases show the principles by which Baxter
attempted to arrive at a conception of Just Price. First,
market or customary price must be taken into account, but
the Just Price may differ from it if the relative bargaining
strength, or wealth, of the two parties should be unequal.
Secondly, charity must be considered, for neither party to
a transaction may ignore the real welfare of the other.
Thirdly, efficiency in business can rightly expect to be
rewarded and inefficiency penalized. There is nothing sentimental about Baxter. He does not seek to set aside economic
laws in favour of a vague universal kindliness. On the
contrary, business as a branch of life is a serious enterprise
with its own technique, only to be engaged upon by those
who have a vocation for it. Its discipline is, and ought to be,
severe, and God must be served by it. But the God thus to
be served is righteous and merciful and therefore the demands
of charity cannot be ignored in economic life.

Not only had the Medieval Church much to say on the
Just Price, but it had also pronounced again and again on
the question of usury. Baxter also has a good deal to say
on lending and borrowing. He says that a poor man might
not rightfully borrow if he knew that he could not repay, or
if he had no reasonable hope of repaying. Under such
circumstances, borrowing is thieving.[3] Baxter then deals with

---

[1] Baxter : *The Christian Directory, Works*, VI, pp. 310-11.
[2] *ibid*, VI, pp. 313f.   [3] *ibid*, VI, p. 315.

raised to some figure short of its full worth. Yes, provided, no contract or custom to the contrary existed, and the tenant had no special claim to consideration. Rents could then be raised provided they were too low before; where the land had undergone improvement, presumably by the landlord; or where there had been a fall in the value of money; or in the case of the value of land having increased owing to growth of population, or other ' accident.' [1] Baxter recognized that varying circumstances prevent one from saying definitely at what figure rents should stand below their market maximum. He pointed out the difference between tenants in efficiency, and the variations between harvests in different years.

A man might take a tenancy, whether of land or a house, over the head of the sitting tenant provided the latter was not unwilling, or if the tenant were justly evicted on grounds of inefficiency or sinfulness, said Baxter. A man might even take a tenancy where the tenant had been unjustly evicted, provided that he had had no hand in the eviction.[2] A rich man ought not to evict in order to increase his own demesne if the tenant were unwilling and would be injured by the eviction, or if such action would lead to depopulation or otherwise injure the Commonwealth. Apart from this there was no Christian objection, and indeed, if ' done in moderation by a pious man may be very convenient ' in keeping the land from being over-populated by too-poor families, and also by resulting in his increasing the number of his servants who, he being a pious man, will benefit spiritually and morally.[3]

In the year of his death, 1691, when he was seventy-six years of age, Baxter wrote his last treatise, *The Poor Husbandman's Advocate to Rich Racking Landlords*,[4] a work marked by an extraordinary vehemence. Although it remained unpublished until 1926, it is important, not only as giving a further indication of Baxter's own views, but as representing much for which he had been working during half a century. This treatise is not concerned with the small yeoman landowner class, nor with tenants of large holdings,

---

[1] Baxter : *The Christian Directory, Works*, VI, p. 359.
[2] *ibid*, VI, p. 362.   [3] *ibid*, VI, p. 359.
[4] Edited by Powicke and published under the title of ' *The Reverend Richard Baxter's Last Treatise*.'

nor even of small if they live near London or any other big market.[1] It is concerned only with the rack-rented man, who had to live entirely off his piece of land, and who must pay his landlord's demands or go. The work is addressed to the wealthy landlords, not that Baxter thought they would, as a class, respond to his appeal. He commenced by referring to a change of custom. No longer were lands let by lease for lives or for a long term of years, as formerly, with a fine at first and then a small yearly rent. Instead, in most counties, yearly rack-rents were now in vogue. This meant that the poor husbandman could only make both ends meet by the most unremitting toil, if indeed then, and that he had no leisure. This lack of leisure was more than a human hardship, for it also conduced to a lack of religion, and hence to a carelessness regarding eternal welfare. The poor husbandmen's condition was important because they formed a very large class; the whole nation lived by them, so that their impoverishment would involve the impoverishment of the nation; their poverty would debase the national spirit, and hence hazard the safety of the nation; and finally, ' Poverty causeth Ignorance . . . and Ignorance . . . wickedness.' This condition of affairs ought to move the landlords to action since they stood to lose most by the depressing of the poor husbandmen, both materially through the inadequate cultivation of the land, and spiritually because their consciences would be troubled, or at all events, they would have to answer for this state of things at the Day of Judgement. The chief cause for the husbandmen's tragic condition was their own sin, otherwise God would have saved them from oppression. But this did not excuse the landlords who failed to regard these poor men as their brethren, over-valuing birth and riches. These landlords loved money, never being satisfied. Their lust for luxurious living needed every penny they could get; they regarded their property as their very own, instead of accepting it as a stewardship. True, the landlords had to provide for themselves and their children. ' I know they must provide for them, and that according to their quality and need. But

---

[1] According to the writer's argument, the higher prices obtainable there would sufficiently cover the increased costs of production which, he said, were due to higher rents.

nothing is due to their posterity that is withheld, or exhorted by oppression, from the poor.'[1]

Baxter's request in face of this indicated his view of a Christian order of society. He said: 'The summe of my request to you is but this . . . that you will . . . sett youre lands to the poore sort of youre tenants at such rates as by their labour and frugality they may comfortably live on, so as not to be necessitated by care for their rents and by tiresome excesses of labour, to be strangers to God's word.'[2] He asked for a reduction of a third in rack-rents, which would be to the advantage of the landlord, since, as things were, many husbandmen, finding they could not make both ends meet, simply abandoned their holdings. He argued for a simpler standard of living, which would not require so large an income, and would indeed be better for the health of the rich. As few landlords were likely to respond to his plea, Baxter finally advised the poor husbandmen how to view their hard lot in the best light. They should beware of those real dangers of poverty, uncharitable thoughts and deceitfulness. They should be thankful for being delivered from the temptations of the rich; for being able to afford only plain food, which is more healthy. However difficult, they must manage somehow to teach their children to read, and to get a Bible and a few good books into the house.

JOHN BUNYAN

In the *Life and Death of Mr. Badman,* Bunyan exposed a number of the petty, dishonest tricks current in business, and was especially hard in his criticism of the pawnbrokers.[3] He dealt with the argument that a man might at all times sell his goods at the highest price obtainable. This could not be right, because always to get the highest price would sometimes involve taking advantage of the buyer's ignorance, necessity, or keen desire. It also involved a denial of charity and of the Golden Rule; it would permit trickery; it would absolve the shopkeeper from his duty of placing his superior business knowledge at the customer's disposal. Finally, it was

---

[1] Baxter: *The Poor Husbandman's Advocate,* p. 37.
[2] *ibid,* p. 38.
[3] Bunyan: *Life and Death of Mr. Badman,* p. 117.

wrong on religious grounds, offending against the glory of God, the name of Christ, and disregarding the Day of Judgement. Yet even Bunyan recognized, if somewhat half-heartedly, that a seller might occasionally try to get the highest price possible, and the buyer the lowest. If, either as buyer or seller, one were dealing with a dishonest man, then let the dishonest man look to himself, yet even so, conscience still had its claims.

RICHARD STEELE

Amongst those ministers deprived in 1662, was Richard Steele (1629-1692), who afterwards gathered a morning congregation at Armourers' Hall, Coleman Street, London. This Dissenting minister wrote *The Tradesman's Calling*, in which he laid down six requisites for the proper managing of a trade or calling, namely, prudence or discretion; diligence; justice; truth or veracity; contentedness; and religiousness. Dealing with the application of the principle of justice to trade, he agreed that while justice implied a rightful price and profit, yet such was often difficult to ascertain exactly. Selling price could not be fixed by the addition of so much to buying price, for the tradesman might have bought a commodity either too dear or especially cheap. Furthermore, ' without doubt a man may take greater gain at one time than at another,' nor could price be fixed simply by the standard of the prices others charged, since they might through necessity or for some other reason, be selling too cheaply. Again, it could not be fixed solely by regard to its previous level since ' commodities ebb and flow, and that which was worth a shilling the last month, may not be worth sixpence this.' Nor could the price charged simply represent a profit sufficient to meet the needs of the vendor and his family, since men's responsibilities vary, while to get the highest price obtainable would not satisfy justice, nor, ' lastly, can the intrinsic worth of a thing be a sufficient rule . . . that in divers commodities cannot be determined, and in many others, the buyer's fancy only makes them valuable.' [1]

---

[1] Steele : *The Tradesman's Calling*, p. 107. This book was revised by Isaac Watts and passed through many editions under the title of ' *The Religious Tradesman*,' the last edition being in 1821—see *D.N.B.*

Lacking a theory of value, Steele falls back on the Golden Rule as the only just method of price fixation, the application of which would forbid taking advantage of another's necessity, or getting an advantage consequent upon the other party's 'unskilfulness.' It would prevent dealing in stolen goods, and demanded that a tradesman should form the habit of 'an honest plainness' in his bargains.[1] While the tradesman should be truthful, 'he is not obliged hereby imprudently to declare always all the Truth he knows . . . though you are bound never to speak a Falsehood, yet you are not bound always to blurt out all the Truth.'[2] The Golden Rule would determine what should be said. Steele agreed in many points with Baxter, and his general conclusion might almost have come from the pages of the *Christian Directory*: 'The market price is generally the surest rule, for that is presumed to be more indifferent than the appetites of particular men. Howbeit in case the seller allow any considerable time to the buyer for the payment of the agreed price, it is lawful enough to advance the rate accordingly; not only because he is thereby depriv'd of the improvement of his money in other traffic, but also runs some hazard of losing it.'[3] Baxter, Steele, and those whose views they may be taken as representing, held that business custom and market conditions, for the most part, offer a reasonable guide in the ethical conduct of affairs, but that none the less, circumstances to do with either party to a transaction would often make this standard insufficient. On such occasions the only real guide was the Golden Rule. Where business practices or customs were obviously wrong, they must, of course, be avoided.[4]

DANIEL DEFOE

Another Dissenter, whose writings had a large public, and who had much to say on economic matters, was Defoe the novelist (1661?-1731). Defoe is of special interest here because, unlike such men as Baxter and Steele, he had been

---

[1] Steele: *op. cit.*, pp. 109-112.
[2] *ibid*, pp. 145f.   [3] *ibid*, pp. 108f.
[4] The Anglican view of the period was not dissimilar, but not usually so detailed. For the seventeenth century, see, *The Whole Duty of Man*, pp. 202-204, for the eighteenth century, see *The New Whole Duty of Man*, pp. 268-270.

in business himself, and also he is a link between the religious outlook on economic life of the seventeenth-century Puritan and the secular outlook of Nonconformists and others in a later period. It is true that although in many ways a pious man, who often adverts to the religious and ethical aspects of economic ideas and practices, his main purpose in writing was not religious. With him, on the contrary, we find that attitude of mind, since to become common, in which business for those engaged in it is regarded as the main pre-occupation of life, in connexion with which religious and ethical principles, though not without importance, do not in practice dominate. Defoe agreed with those moralists who taught the serious importance of the use of time. 'Time is no more to be unemploy'd, than it is to be ill employ'd.' [1] In the right use of our time three ends should be regarded : the necessities of nature; the duties of religion, or things relating to a future life; and the duties of the present life, one's Business or Calling. Concerning the religious duties, 'They ought not by any means to be thrust out of their places, and yet they ought to be kept in their places too.' [2] Here we see the beginning of a separation of religion and business activities, for although Defoe was only referring to religious duties in the narrower sense, such as attendance at public worship and private prayer, he had departed from the governing principle, *laborare est orare,* and the way was open for the development of a double standard of morality. This double standard was, in fact, quietly assumed in a good deal of what he has to say.

Defoe offered the young Tradesman advice as to how to act if he finds his business failing. He should not delay too long in going bankrupt. 'If you see you are going down, and that the hazard of going on is doubtful, I say, *Break in time.'* [3] The object of this is to preserve a reputation for honesty and to obtain better terms from creditors—indeed some creditors might very well be found willing to give further, and even extended credit. Elsewhere, Defoe advocated the setting up of a Court of Inquiries to which every man who found himself pressed by his affairs so that he could not carry on his

---

[1] Defoe : *The Complete English Tradesman,* p. 50.
[2] *ibid,* p. 50.
[3] *ibid,* p. 78. He could speak from experience, having been a bankrupt himself.

business could apply. The Commissioners of this Court should then send their officer to take possession of the house and goods of the applicant, and make an inventory. The bankrupt, according to this scheme, must provide an accurate account of his estate, real and personal, and the Commissioners, having verified the account, must return to the applicant five per cent. of his estate and give him a full discharge from all his creditors, the balance of ninety-five per cent. to be fairly divided amongst the creditors.[1]

Defoe also dealt with the question of business morality. An honest man and an honest tradesman might sometimes be differentiated; in fact, a tradesman could be considered honest even if he did give himself some ‘ liberty,’ provided that he did not go too far. What the writer had in mind particularly was the old question of price, and he argued that there was nothing wrong in a man asking somewhat above his minimum figure. He thus referred to ‘ the Quakers (who) stood for a time in the contrary practice . . . but time and the necessities of trade made them wise . . . indeed it is the buyers that make this custom necessary.’[2] Defoe has taken Baxter’s position, although rather cynically, and pushed it further. He asserted that in reality trade lying was not the tradesman’s fault. It was the buyers who ‘ begin the work, and give the occasion. . . . The Buyer telling us . . . that everything is worse than it is, forces us, in justifying its true value, to tell them it is better than it is.’[3] He ignored the fact that tradesmen were themselves buyers as well as sellers.

---

[1] Defoe: *Essay on Projects,* in, *The Earlier . . . Works . . . Defoe,* pp. 117-119. Steele, however, who also has something to say on this question, regarded bankruptcy with grave suspicion because of the possibilities it might afford for unethical conduct. He roundly condemned ‘ breaking upon design. And that is, when a Tradesman conceals an estate, and counterfeits a failure, compounds with his creditors, induces them to accept a part of their due debt for the whole.’—Steele, *op. cit.,* p. 103. Isaac Watts asserts that the Dissenters of the early eighteenth century thought no worse of bankruptcy than their neighbours. For one thing they had become too fond of pleasure and they neglected their business—Dale: *op. cit.,* p. 557. The London Yearly Meeting of 1759 sent out an Epistle advising that where a Quaker had made a composition with his creditors, and was legally discharged from paying the remainder, he must yet endeavour in the future to repay the whole, and keep down his standard of living meanwhile. Then the Yearly Meeting of 1782 warned ‘ Friends in struggling or embarrassed circumstances . . . to be particularly careful not to pay one creditor in preference to another,’—Society of Friends: *The Book of Christian Discipline,* p. 123.
[2] Defoe: *The Complete English Tradesman,* p. 227.   [3] *ibid,* p. 252.

This writer was as much against pleasure as any orthodox Puritan, but for a different reason. For the tradesman, a constant application of head and hand was demanded by his calling, and was therefore his duty. 'Pleasures and diversions may be innocent in themselves which are not so to him: there are very few things in the world that are simply evil, but things are made circumstantially evil when they are not so in themselves.'[1] The writer did not think that business should be isolated from a morality based upon religion. Economics must pay some attention to ethics, and in the long run such attention would pay, for 'nothing but probity will support credit.'[2] Circumstances, however, being what they are, conduct that in other realms would be unethical is allowable, because inevitable, in economic life. The same code of ethics cannot govern business as other things, but departures from it must be few, and thoroughly justified by circumstances. So a man, with care, might hope to keep his soul without losing his business.

John Wesley

Wesley and Baxter were probably the most influential leaders in their respective centuries. Both possessed systematic minds, but presented their ideas on economic subjects in different ways. Wesley produced his much more as isolated judgements than was the case with Baxter, and while the ideas of both were the product of definite theological opinions, those of Wesley were less liable to modification. Without explicitly admitting it, Baxter seemed to feel that in an imperfect world some compromise was inevitable, and if inevitable, not wrong. Defoe, as we have seen, simply went a step further by admitting this compromise bluntly and claiming for it ethical validity. Very different, however, is the attitude of Wesley. When he faced circumstances running counter to principle, he saw only one thing to be done: the circumstances must at all costs be changed. Opportunist in matters of organization and administration, in matters of principle Wesley was adamant.

The nearest approach to a systematic statement of the great Methodist's economic views is to be found in his sermon on

---

[1] Defoe: *The Complete English Tradesman*, p. 97.　　[2] *ibid*, p. 348.

'The Use of Money,' and in his eighth sermon in the series on the Sermon on the Mount.[1] The former is so illuminating that an analysis is here given. Wesley, in his introduction to this sermon, explained that the term 'Mammon' meant riches, or money, and was said to be unrighteous because of the unrighteous way in which it was frequently procured, and the unrighteous way in which money, honestly obtained, was generally employed. The preacher was quite clear that, so far from money being evil in itself, it could be an instrument of the greatest good. 'In the hands of (God's) children, it is food for the hungry, drink for the thirsty, raiment for the naked. . . . By it we may supply the place of an husband to the widow, and of a father to the fatherless . . . it may be eyes to the blind, as feet to the lame; yea, a lifter up from the gates of death.'[2] As money had such great power, it became of the first importance to know how to employ it rightly.

'Gain all you can.' This was not only permissive, but obligatory. Nevertheless, since life was more important than money, wealth might be obtained only in ways that would not impair life or health. Therefore, one should not enter or continue in an unhealthy occupation. Nor might one engage in any occupation involving sin, such as smuggling, which was a form of theft, or any business in which a competence could be obtained only by dishonest means. No business is lawful, in the conduct of which another man was economically harmed. Therefore, money must not be lent at such an interest 'as even the laws of our country forbid,' which maxim, Wesley said, would forbid pawnbroking. Goods must not be sold below the market price; another man's trade must not be deliberately harmed; nor may we entice from him his servants or workmen. No business is lawful which resulted in the physical harm of another, e.g. spirituous

[1] 'The Use of Money' is the title of a sermon on Luke xvi. 9, 'I say unto you, Make to yourselves friends of the mammon of unrighteousness; that, when ye fail, they may receive you into everlasting habitations.' Its three divisions are famous, namely, Gain all you can; Save all you can; Give all you can—but what he has to say under each heading is by no means so well known. See *Sermons*, II, pp. 311-327. For the sermon in the series on the Sermon on the Mount, see *Sermons*, I, pp. 473-494.

[2] *Sermons*, II, p. 314. For similar sentiment, see Whitefield: *Works*, IV, p. 384. The idea here expressed was not uncommonly taught at the time.

liquors. On similar grounds surgeons, apothecaries, and physicians were condemned if they did not cure people as quickly as they could. No business resulting in harm to another's soul can be justified. Therefore let all beware who have to do with taverns or any ' places of public fashionable diversion.' Engaged in some calling free from these objections, a man must use all possible diligence, in gaining all he can.[1] Wesley finished this section by insisting that the Christian, as such, ought to be a more efficient *entrepreneur* than the worldling. He demanded that a man should use all his mental powers in the planning of his business, and especially warned against following old methods just because they were customary. ' It is a shame for a Christian not to improve upon *them* in whatever he takes in hand. You should be continually learning, from the experience of others, or from your own experience, reading, and reflection, to do everything you have to do better to-day than you did yesterday.'[2]

' Save all you can.' To save implies not to waste, therefore unnecessary expense must be watched.[3] It was wasteful to indulge the pleasures of sense; especially in regard to food.[4] Expensive clothes, needless ornaments, unnecessary or costly furniture, expensive gardens, were also wasteful. So, too, were costly works of art and expensive books. Money must not be spent to gratify pride. Parents should no more spend money on their children in any of the above ways than on themselves.

---

[1] Wesley fixed the times of week-day services with an eye to the calls of industry. He had to meet the criticism that his movement would prove contrary to the needs of employers by encouraging men to remain away from their work. In reply, he pointed out that the Methodist preaching hours were 5 a.m. and 7 p.m., that is, before and after the usual hours of work—*Journal*, III, p. 240. Gradually, people discovered that Methodism tended to produce better workmen, and did not interfere with the normal hours of labour. They also found that when a man became a Methodist he rarely afterwards became a charge on the parish—Matthew Lumb : *A Few Animadversions upon a Pamphlet, entitled ' an Earnest and affectionate address to the people called Methodists,'* p. 48; Richard Chew : *James Everett,* p. 9. (Both references quoted in Warner : *The Wesleyan Movement in the Industrial Revolution,* p. 167.)

[2] *Sermons*, II, p. 320.

[3] *Methodist Minutes* (1862 edit.), p. 53. The Conference of 1765 asked, ' Are our people good economists? ' and enjoined, ' In public and private, enlarge on economy as a branch of religion.'

[4] *Sermons*, II, p. 321.

'Give all you can.' Wesley argued that to leave money in the Bank was equivalent to burying it in the earth; and not to use money is tantamount to throwing it away. As we are but God's stewards we must act accordingly. God has said, 'in the most clear and express terms' how wealth is to be employed. The faithful steward will use his money in the following way: first he will provide for himself, then for his wife, then for his children, then for his servants or any others belonging to his household. If a surplus remains, 'as you have opportunity, do good unto all men.' If a man is in doubt as to the ethical aspect of his expenditure, let him inquire if in that particular expense he is behaving as a steward ought, if he is acting according to Biblical precepts, if this expense can be made a sacrifice to God, and if he can be confident of receiving a reward for this use of his money at the 'resurrection of the just.'

Finally, Wesley demanded that each person should render to God, not a tenth, third, or half of his money, but all. In his last paragraph, he characteristically joined together the getting, and the getting rid, of money: 'No more sloth! Whatsoever your hand findeth to do, do it with all your might! No more waste. . . . No more covetousness! But employ whatever God has entrusted you with, in doing good.'[1]

In his sermon in the series on the Sermon on the Mount, based on the passage in Matthew vi. 19-23, Wesley repeated in other words much of what is contained in the above. This sermon makes clear, however, that by his injunctions to give away the surplus above the needs of one's own household, he did not believe a business could be carried on without capital. He said that it was quite right to accumulate sufficient working capital 'for the carrying on our worldly business, in such a measure and degree as is sufficient to' owe no man anything and to have enough to meet the needs of dependents.[2] This sermon contains a stern warning to the rich, culminating in the cry, 'But there is at hand a greater trouble. . . . Thou art to die!'[3] But the common sense of Wesley recognized here that a man might be rich through no fault of his own but because of an 'over-ruling

[1] Sermons, II, pp. 326f.   [2] ibid, I, p. 481.   [3] ibid, I, p. 486.

providence.' In fact, however, most rich men rob God by their wasting of His goods, and *ipso facto,* rob the poor. Wesley was not only against speculation, but did not approve any unnecessary changing of estates, real or personal. The faithful steward ought ' not to sell either his houses or lands, or principal stock, be it more or less, unless some peculiar circumstance should require it; (nor) desire or endeavour to increase, any more than to squander it away in vanity; but to employ it wholly to those wise and reasonable purposes for which his Lord has lodged it in his hands.' [1] Providence, that is to say, is shown, not only in the distribution of wealth, but even in the particular form in which a person may have it.

It should be remembered that these *Standard Sermons* were preached again and again over a period exceeding half a century, no doubt varying somewhat in form and content in different times and places, but substantially the same.[2] They were not isolated utterances, but represent Wesley's normal and constant teaching. Probably a large proportion of his followers heard the two above sermons at some time or other, and some several times, while the ideas in them would become common currency in the sermons of his ever-growing band of preachers.

Employers, Employees, and Employment

It will be convenient to treat what the Nonconformists had to say on questions of employment as a whole, rather than under each writer separately, since these questions do not loom so large in their writings as questions more obviously dealing with business morality. In discussions on employment in the period with which we are dealing, the relations between masters and servants generally took a large place, and Nonconformist Divines also had a good deal to say on this point. Baxter urged that it was the duty of the masters to see that their servants were neither idle nor overworked, while they, the servants, must not be required to do any unlawful thing. The duties of servants towards their masters lay in trustworthiness in word and act, and especially in being trustworthy in buying and selling. Neither

---

[1] *Sermons*, I, p. 492.

[2] *ibid,* I, Preface, p. 29—Wesley in 1746 said these sermons ' contain the substance' of his preaching for the previous eight or nine years.

should they complain at simple food as long as it was whole-some, nor want an idle or easy life. They should do every-thing in obedience to God, from whom alone they were to expect reward.[1]   Masters should remember that in order to get good servants they must be good masters.[2]   Servants, on their part, ought to realize that because of the scarcity of good servants, they would be able to make their choice of places provided that they excelled in work, trustworthiness, and obedience.[3]

Defoe dealt at length with the 'servant problem' in London.   He asserted that the wages of domestic servants had advanced from thirty or forty shillings to as much as six, seven, or eight pounds a year.   Servants coming from the country were quickly spoilt, wages being forced up by a sort of unofficial 'trades union.'   They lived extravagantly and often immorally.   He complained bitterly at the petty thieving and pilfering of which, he alleged, they were guilty, and he particularly denounced those upper servants who drew commissions from the tradesmen with whom they dealt on behalf of their employers.[4]   The remedy Defoe proposed was that a servant, on leaving a position, should have a written character, and none should be hired without.[5]

Bunyan, speaking of masters and apprentices, indicated ways in which an apprentice might be led astray: by being made to work too hard with inadequate time for worship; by the master allowing immoral books or talk in the house; by the wickedness of fellow-servants; by hypocrisy or dis-honesty on the part of the master.[6]

Whitefield, in his *Prayers on Several Occasions,* put these words into the mouth of a servant: 'Give me grace . . . to obey my master . . . not with eye-service . . . but with singleness of heart, as unto Christ . . . make me patient of reproof, willing to be taught, and subject with all fear and godly reverence, not only to the good and gentle, but also to the froward.'[7]

[1] Baxter: *The Poor Man's Family Book, Works,* XIX, pp. 498f.
[2] Baxter: *The Christian Directory, Works,* III, p. 209.
[3] *ibid,* III, p. 47.
[4] Defoe: *Everybody's Business is Nobody's Business,* pp. 4, 8.
[5] *ibid,* p. 23.
[6] Bunyan: *Life and Death of Mr. Badman,* pp. 42f.
[7] Whitefield: *Works,* IV, pp. 471-3.

The Wesleys had a number of hymns suitable for masters and servants,[1] which show their attitude to have been that the master was responsible for the well-being of his servants, which included their proper governance, reasonable comfort and happiness, and their moral and spiritual development. The servant, on his part, owed willing obedience to his master, even if the latter proved to be a tyrant. To some extent the master stood *in loco dei*. Masters and servants were brethren—with God there is no respect of persons, for Christ died for all.[2]

In a pamphlet of 1773, 'Thoughts on the Present Scarcity of Provisions,'[3] Wesley dealt with what he considered to be the causes and remedies of the high prices and dearth of employment then obtaining. He said that the poverty and semi-starvation, which he had himself observed up and down the kingdom, was caused by unemployment, itself due to bad trade. The bad trade was the result of the high price of provisions which left so many people with nothing to spare for any other purchases after they had bought food. Nor was it provisions only which were so dear; rents and the general price level were high too. The basic reason for all this dearness was the high taxation on nearly everything, and the high taxes were due to the National Debt. Therefore half the National Debt should be discharged, thereby saving £2,000,000 per annum. This could be achieved 'by abolishing all useless pensions, as fast as those who now enjoy them die.' He added, however, that he did not expect that this would be done. Dealing, in this pamphlet, with the more detailed causes of high food prices, Wesley examined in turn certain of the principal commodities. 'Bread-corn' was dear because of the immense quantities used for distilling; oats because the number of horses had quadrupled in the last few years; and, 'as the dearness of grain of one

[1] See *Hymns for the Use of Families*, 1767, Hymns numbered 134, 135, 136, 137, 139, 140, 141, 142, 144.
[2] cf. Ephesians vi. 5-9, also Ames: *De Conscientia*, V, pp. 232f, 'De mutua obligatione inter dominos et servos, qua et qualis sit? . . . Subjectionem et obedientiam istam debent non tantum bonis et moderatis dominis, set etiam pravis et duris. 1 Peter ii. 18.' For similar Anglican attitude on this question, for the seventeenth century see *The Whole Duty of Man*, pp. 268-272, and for the eighteenth century see *The New Whole Duty of Man*, pp. 236-241.
[3] *Works*, XI, pp. 50ff.

kind will always raise the price of another, so whatever cause
the dearness of wheat and oats, must raise the price of barley
too.' Beef and mutton were dear because so many farmers,
especially in the North, had become horse-breeders, as it paid
better, the horses being annually exported by thousands to
France. Pork, poultry, and eggs were dear owing to the
disappearance of the small farmer 'because of the
monopolizing of farms. . . . The land which was some years
ago divided between ten or twenty little farmers . . . is now
generally engrossed by one great farmer. . . . Every one of
these little farmers kept a few swine, with some quantity of
poultry.' Luxury was another cause of high prices. Land
itself was dear, because, owing to the advance of other prices,
gentlemen needed a greater income, and so raised their rents.
'And then the farmer paying an higher rent for the land,
must have an higher price for the produce of it. This again
tends to raise the price of land. And so the wheel runs
round.' The remedy proposed for this state of things was
to reverse the process. People must have work in order not
to starve, therefore trade must be made to improve. This
would be possible if distilling were prohibited; if more sheep
and cattle were kept; if the number of horses were reduced
(by taxation); if no farms were to be let above £100 per
annum, so as to bring back the small farmer; and if luxury
were repressed.

In this pamphlet we see Wesley's concern for the poor.
He spent a life time in the practice of charity, but perceived
that the solution of the problem, as distinct from its palliation,
was economic. As an economist he was defective, arguing
that high rents cause high prices and assuming that price-levels
can be altered and volume of employment increased without
regard to foreign trade (except for the export of horses). He
did notice the important social and economic change which
was passing over the land owing to the disappearance of the
yeoman cultivators. Like many of his contemporaries, he
emphasized luxury as a cause of economic trouble, while he,
Tory as he was, anticipated to some extent the Radical
agitation of 1783 and onwards.

Five years later, in 1778, we find Wesley writing in quite
a different strain, at a time of great excitement and even

panic. He published, ' A Serious Address to the People of England, with regard to the state of the Nation.'[1] In this he argued that England, although at war, was prospering. Cattle and vegetables were being produced in undiminished quantities. Population had increased within the last twenty years, and during the same period, he said hundreds of thousands of acres of land hitherto reckoned as unprofitable had been tilled. He remarked especially on the great increase of the Irish trade. 'Let none deceive you. . . . You are compassed with liberty, peace, and plenty.' Wesley was always against anything in the nature of panic, and this second pamphlet would seem to have been in part inspired by the desire to contribute something in face of the dangerous state of the country at the time.

[1] *Works,* XI, pp. 134ff.

Chapter VIII

NONCONFORMITY AND POVERTY

The Nonconformist Approach
to the Problem of Poverty

SIXTEENTH-CENTURY England saw a not inconsiderable growth in wealth, but the discovery and transportation to Europe in that century of the precious metals of the New World had been followed by a long-continued rise in prices. Although wages had gradually risen, the time-lag combined with the monopoly prices demanded for many of the necessaries of life had involved hardship. In the seventeenth century came the Civil War, bringing a large increase of taxation, and the burden of free quarter, combined with the bad harvests of the middle of that century, depressed the condition of the labourers further, and increased the numbers of those on the poverty line. Religious and political changes increased the unrest, in which some of the Puritans were implicated. A Communistic movement appeared under Everard and Winstanley, and the latter became the leader of the English Communists. Winstanley advocated that property must be the common possession of all; that all in office should be elected annually; that production should be both individual and co-operative, and productive work be enforced if necessary on all; and that education should be universal, technical education being included.[1]

There was in the Puritan tradition regarding the poor another and very different strain from this revolutionary one, a bourgeois view associated with the trading and professional classes, some members of which, like Sir Matthew Hale, really desired to help the poor, but without radical change in the existing social and economic structure. There also developed a third strain, represented by such men as Bellers, who,

[1] Winstanley: *The Law of Freedom*, pp. 18, 23, 83, and Chap. 5 on education.

without being in the least revolutionary in the political sense, sought to change social life by devising means, not merely of relieving all the poor, but of banishing poverty.

Early in our period, the Nonconformist connexion with poverty was a personal one, through persecution, of which the Quakers bore the major part. Many Friends were ruined, or seriously embarrassed financially, by the prosecutions in respect of non-payment of tithes and other Church demands. Between 1696 and 1736, it is calculated that 1,180 such prosecutions took place, 302 persons suffering imprisonment. Some of the seizures were ruinous, amounting to twenty or thirty times the original demand, while the legal expenses of defence were often great.[1] Thus did many Quakers gain an intimate knowledge of the life of the poor as a consequence of their own conscientious attitude. Then the ejectment of ministers in 1662 and 1663; the fines and imprisonment which were widely imposed on Dissenters; and the economic limitations which resulted from the application of parts of the Clarendon Code, all brought home the fact of poverty to the Nonconformists as such. In Methodism, too, there was a deeply personal contact with poverty, on the one hand because most of the converts were themselves of the poorer classes, and on the other because of the deliberate policy of Wesley that he and his preachers should be poor men.[2] The preacher was worthy of his hire; he had no claim to more. At the same time, moralists, of whom Baxter was so outstanding an example, brought their own individual point of view to bear on the traditional attitude towards the poor.

Richard Baxter realized that not only was religion of importance as a sanction for charity, but, on the other hand, the relief of the poor was a pre-requisite if they were to be able to practise religion. Religion and charity were to some extent mutually dependent. 'While pinching wants are calling away your mind . . . when there is a family to provide for, a discontented wife and children to satisfy, rents and debts, and demands unpaid, it must be an excellent Christian that can live contentedly, and cast all his useless

[1] Besse: *A Brief Account of many of the Prosecutions of the People call'd Quakers*, 'index of the number of Prosecutions,' also, pp. 6, 8, 9, 13, 20, 22, 35, and others.
[2] *Supra*, pp. 53ff.

and glebe lands to the poor, and turn the great houses, abbeys, churches, and Whitehall itself into almshouses, and he would have all fines and amercements, and great gifts given to great men, devoted to the relief of poverty.' [1]

In 1660, a Westmoreland Quaker schoolmaster named Thomas Lawson, addressed an appeal to Parliament,[2] in which he advocated a statistical inquiry concerning the poor, the setting up of Employment Exchanges, and that the Courts should see that the poor were neither neglected nor misused. The statistics were to be by parishes, of the old, impotent, and of young children. Collections, he urged, should be made so as to supplement the earnings of those whose incomes were insufficient. For the unemployed, each parish, or other authority should arrange with some clothier or other tradesman, to provide work for ten or more unemployed, who should be forced, if necessary, to work. The Employment Exchange, which Lawson called a ' poor man's office,' was to act as a place where handicraftsmen and labourers wanting work, and where employers wanting workmen, might inquire; where boys might inquire of masters to whom to be apprenticed, and where those wanting servants could come. Here maids fit to become apprentices, or covenant-servants, or those wanting such, might inquire; none to be put to service, however, unless they were first taught to spin, knit, sew, or some other work. At this office, also, any who were destitute could apply in order that means might be taken to supply their needs. All, Lawson pleaded, should have the right of access to justices and others if they wished to complain of the neglect or misuse of the poor. Judges of Assizes and Sessions ought to see that the laws for the relief of the poor were being worked. The poor should not have their personal liberty restricted nor be constrained in any way until means had been used to supply their wants. This scheme of Lawson's showed a combination of the old ideas and methods concerning the poor, with a modern approach.

---

[1] Braithwaite : *The Second Period of Quakerism*, pp. 558f.
[2] T.L. : *An Appeal to the Parliament concerning the Poor, that there may not be a Beggar in England.* For some reference to Lawson, see Bellasco : *Note on the Labour Exchange Idea in the Seventeenth Century* —The Economic Journal (Economic History Supplement), Vol. I, pp. 275-279. Also, Braithwaite : *The Second Period of Quakerism*, p. 559.

The next Nonconformist of any note to deal with the problem, was the Baptist, Richard Haines, of Horsham, Sussex, the author of at least seven pamphlets on the subject of poor relief and employment, published between 1674 and 1680. He observed that of recent years everyone had become poorer,[1] and considered the causes of poverty to be the decline in exportable commodities combined with an increase in the import of expensive goods. Unless the balance of trade could be restored, 'then of necessity out goes Money, and in comes Poverty.'[2] The remedies suggested were the raising of new manufactures combined with the reduction, or prohibition, of imported goods, especially linen, brandy, salt and salt-petre, and iron. Haines gave it as his opinion that the poor state of the iron manufacture accounted for the destruction of timber as wooded land was being converted into tillage. In general, he aimed at the restoration of the woollen and linen manufactures, his special contribution here being an invention for spinning, whereby, it was claimed, 'one man may turn fifty spinning-wheels, which shall serve 100 persons to spin at once : so that they shall have nothing to do but employ both hands to draw Tire from the Distaff, and to earn 9d. a day as easily as now they can 6d.'[3] He advocated the construction of a 'Working-Hospital' in every county, by means of which he hoped to increase the production of linen, lighten the burden of poor relief, restrain and reform beggars and vagrants, and commence the moral and industrial education of children. These county workhouses, according to his plan, would be run by committees consisting of representatives of all the parishes with overseers.[4] He thought by this means to avoid financial abuse and maltreatment of the poor.[5] From his writing it appears that he had an interview with Charles II, about 1677,

---

[1] Haines: *The Prevention of Poverty*, p. 1.
[2] Haines: *ibid*, p. 12.
[3] Philo-Anglicus, Gent: *Bread for the Poor*, p. 5. Haines claimed that 'the invention of these Engines is wholly mine, and if they prove effectual, I hope I shall not be deprived of receiving some benefit thereof; because I am so free as in effect to discover it beforehand'—Haines: *Proposals for building . . . Working Alms House*, p. 6. Apparently they did not prove effectual, little or nothing having been heard of them.
[4] Haines: *Proposals for building . . . Working Alms House*, pp. 2f; see also, Haines: *A Method of Government . . . Alms Houses*.
[5] Haines: *A Model of Government for the Good of the Poor.*

per annum for its poor children, as follows, £20 salary for a woman to teach spinning and reading; £5 rent of large room in which the teaching was to be done; £25 for the purchase of hemp and flax; £25 for the payment to the children for their work at 1d. per 600 yards of yarn; £15 for weaving this yarn and whitening the cloth made from it; £8 for the wheels and reels used; and £2 for the Trustees' Annual Dinner. The cloth made was to be distributed to the poor as needed. The chief point Firmin has in the above is that children, by this teaching, should be prepared to earn their own livings.

Firmin's second main proposal concerned the older people. These he wanted to be supplied with hemp and flax to be spun in their own homes. He was against putting them into a workhouse, to which few would willingly come, but he agreed that workhouses were right for vagrants and sturdy beggars who must be disciplined. He advocated the raising of higher duties on imported linen to encourage the home manufacture.

No less important than Firmin was the Quaker, John Bellers (1655?-1725), whose interests and writings covered a wide field, including poor relief, education, international politics, and theology.[1] He forms a link between the Quaker philanthropists of the eighteenth century and the dynamic leaders of the seventeenth, such as Fox, Penn, and many others. His principal proposal was the foundation of agricultural colonies, called 'Colleges of Industry,' a convenient size for each of which is suggested as 300 persons, of whom 200 would be sufficient to provide for the wants of the whole number, leaving the labour of the remaining 100 as a profit. Bellers thought not only that his colleges were workable, but that they would have certain definite advantages over competitors, in that there would be saved shopkeepers and all useless (sic) trades, with their servants and dependents; lawsuits; bad debts; dear bargains; loss of time for want of work; beggars; much houseroom; firing, cooking, brewing, baking; much fetching and carrying of work and provisions; goods damaged in making, which although they

---

[1] A useful article on Bellers by P. S. Belasco appeared in 'Economica,' June 1925, pp. 165-174.

could not be sold, could be worn by members of the College. Similarly, he argued that the college land would have advantages in that the labour of the tradesmen, as well as that of the husbandmen, would be available; more cattle would be kept, and hence there would be more manure; there would be no disputes between landlords and tenants; the mechanics could help at harvest-time.

Bellers proposed to finance his scheme by the issue of shares, with a maximum voting power for large shareholders of five votes, and with a committee of twelve to act as directors. Characteristically, Bellers, who combined a real concern for the poor with an understanding of the point of view of the rich, urged that such Colleges would have definite advantages for their Founders, and for rich men generally. Investors, he argued, would get a good return on their money (for the reasons advanced in the previous paragraph), and furthermore, ' An £100 per annum in such a College, I suppose will maintain ten times as many people as £100 in Almshouses, or Hospitals; because the provision and manufacture raised from £100 per annum land is worth ten times the rent; as the farmer raiseth yearly three times his rent, and the mechanics make their work worth three or four times what it was in the Farmers Hands.' [1] The advantages contemplated for the members of these communities (' Poor Collegians ') were that from being poor they would become rich, i.e. they would have all things needful; they would be encouraged to, instead of discouraged from, marriage; and they would only have to do a reasonable day's work, without worry, with no loss of earnings through bad bargains, bad debts or lawsuits. At sixty years of age, they could be made overseers, more or less retired. Also, ' the regular life in the College, with abatement of worldly cares, with an easy honest labour and religious instructions, may make it a nursery and school of virtue. The poor thus in a College, will be a Community something like the example of primitive Christianity.' Bellers wanted the poor to have an incentive to work, other than that supplied by dire necessity. He had three ruling principles : the poor ought not to be regarded as a nuisance, but as ordinary human beings; it is only want of good

---

[1] Bellers : *Proposals for Raising a College of Industry,* p. 12.

management which prevents them earning more than enough for their own living; and their moral and spiritual welfare must not be overlooked.[1] He calculated that at the end of the seventeenth century there were 500,000 poor in the Kingdom, and that every 500 people were capable of earning £3,000 per annum more than necessary to keep them. He was quite sure that the poor would cease to be poor when their labour was properly directed. In fact, ' it's only the labour of the poor that increases the riches of a nation, if their imployments are in due proportion; yet there may be too many traders in a country for the number of labourers.' Apparently, Bellers regarded markets as capable of unlimited expansion, even though he realized that the commercial side might be easily overcrowded. Unemployment, he regarded as a problem of organization, and it was a function of the rich to supply the necessary wise direction of labour. By this means Bellers, with some ingenuity, proposed an escape for the rich from the moral and spiritual danger of their riches, which at the same time should deliver the poor from the evil effects of their poverty. The rich, excused by their wealth from personal labour, must devote their time to organizing the labour of others.[2] So the stewardship of wealth becomes a stewardship of time, and a man might save his soul and his estates by the same course of action. Elsewhere,[3] Bellers apportions to the rich another function, that of acting as a Health Insurance Fund. ' It's as much the duty of the poor to labour when they are able, as it is for the rich to help them when they are sick.'

The College of Industry provided for its own sick people

[1] *The College of Industry* was published in 1696, and was followed for years by a stream of tracts and works, addressed variously to Quakers, Royal Commissioners, the Lord Mayor and Aldermen of London, Parliament, and others. Contemporary Quaker Minutes show that he had a large influence amongst the members of his own body during his lifetime—see *F.H.S.*, 1915, pp. 165-171. After his death, nothing was heard about him for nearly a century, until Francis Place read the *Proposals for Raising a College of Industry*, which he promptly introduced to Robert Owen, who circulated 1,000 copies of this tract. Bellers is again referred to in Karl Marx's *Das Capital*, and since then in the histories of Socialism—see Beer: *A History of British Socialism*, I, pp. 71, 75, and 174f.

[2] Bellers: *Essays about the Poor, Manufactures, Trade, Plantations, and Immorality* . . . p. 15.

[3] Bellers: *An Essay towards the Improvement of Physick* . . . *With an Essay for Imploying the Able Poor.*

—one physician and six nurses to be kept for 300 members. Bellers now considers what can be done for the sick and incapable poor in general, and proposes hospitals for the poor to be built in or near London, one hospital for the blind, one for incurables, and one doctor at least for the poor in each county hundred or city parish. He still has an eye to running his schemes at a profit, and therefore argues that wherever possible the inmates of these hospitals should be put to work. Employing his usual argument that labour can earn much more than rents can produce, he suggests that the City of London, to which this is addressed, should employ the poor to work on their hospital lands, and with the crops produced to supply the hospitals.[1] He also wanted some enclosure of forests and commons to be effected. 'If they were made liable to be divided by a writ of partition, in proportion to everyone's right, much of those lands would be greatly improved, and many of those poor bred to a more industrious and honest way of living, and each of them having a piece of land added to their cottage to work upon, they will be of more value (when so inclosed) than their Commonage is to them now.'[2]

Bellers makes a computation of annual losses due to the poor being inadequately employed, which is of interest as giving his estimate of the population which he puts at the figure of 7,000,000. He assumes that one in every fourteen men, women, and children are not in work. He then assumes that they might, if proposals such as his were widely acted upon, each earn on average 6d. per diem (Sundays excluded), or £3,900,000 per annum. To this he would add twelve pence per head per week, representing the sum saved from the parish rate and private charity, or £1,300,000 per annum. Thus he aims at an annual sum of £5,200,000 accruing as a result of a proper organization of the labour of the poor. He is constantly reiterating to all sorts of people and bodies his belief that all the poor could be put to remunerative work.[3]

Daniel Defoe, dealing with questions of poor relief and employment, asserted that in actual fact there was a shortage

---

[1] Bellers: *An Essay towards the Improvement of Physick . . . With an Essay for Imploying the Able Poor.*
[2] *ibid,* p. 40.   [3] *ibid,* p. 43.

of labour, which was proved by the high level of wages, and the difficulty of obtaining recruits for the Army, while it was the luxury, sloth, and pride of the working classes that caused their poverty.[1] He argued against workhouses engaging in spinning, weaving, and manufacturing wool, their usual occupations, on the ground that these occupations were already in the hands of private enterprise, and therefore a workhouse, instead of providing more work, simply transferred what work there was from one body of people to another. It was useless to increase production without increasing consumption.[2] The solution of the problem of the poor lay, not in the provision of charitable institutions—'public nuisances'—but in an adequate regulation of the poor, whereby their luxurious and lazy habits, and their spendthrift natures might be changed.[3]

John Wesley was much concerned with the poor from his Oxford days. His personal charities, in the aggregate during his long lifetime, were very considerable, while in addition, he organized and directed the charity of many others. From his evangelical conversion in 1738 to his death in 1791, he was in almost constant touch with the poor, both those who were destitute and those normally living on the poverty line. Like so many others, he tried his hand at providing employment for the poor, and he also, in 1746, started a loan society for small tradesmen.[4] A Methodist, John Gardner, in 1785, started the Strangers' Friend Society to help those who were afflicted and without friends, a movement which rapidly spread throughout Methodism.[5]

The Nonconformist bodies in their charitable work generally proceeded on three principles : they held that relief of the poor and suffering was a Christian duty; that such relief must be efficient and not merely well-intentioned; and also that the gospel required personal attendance and service of the poor, the sick, and prisoners, as well as pecuniary

[1] Defoe : *Giving Alms No Charity*, pp. 9, 12, 24, 25. This book was of considerable influence, and was written in opposition to a Bill put forward by Sir Humphrey Mackworth to establish parochial manufactories—see Wright : *Life of Defoe*, p. 108.
[2] *ibid*, pp. 15-17.
[3] *ibid*, p. 27.
[4] Blanshard : *op. cit.*, p. 85; Warner : *op. cit.*, pp. 220f; *Letters*, II, p. 309; *W.H.S.*, III, pp. 197f and V, p. 213.
[5] Tyerman : *Life and Times . . . Wesley*, III, p. 253; *Letters*, VII, p. 308.

contributions. In accordance with these principles, charity might be wisely exercised in a variety of ways, some of which Gouge suggests—lending stock to such as might need it; forgiving debtors; visitation and help of those in prison.[1] Baxter, in his list of eminent works of charity, included the fitting out of poor men's sons as apprentices and the provision of 'stocks of money or yearly rents, to be lent for five, or six, or seven years to young tradesmen at their setting up.'[2] Firmin wished that the City of London itself could be persuaded to provide a stock and suitable place to act as a pawnshop.[3] Reference has already been made to his connexion with the hospitals. Bellers, too, had urged physicians to be charitable in their attendance on poor patients.[4] In the Methodist societies, organized sick relief appeared early. In 1741, a group of voluntary workers was engaged under Wesley in regular sick visitation.[5] Special rules were issued by Conference for visitors to the sick. A free dispensary was established in London in 1746 and continued until 1754, when it had to be given up owing to expense.[6] Dispensaries for the poor became fairly numerous in the eighteenth century.[7]

NONCONFORMISTS AND THEIR OWN POOR.

Having considered the attitude of the Nonconformists towards the poor in general, we may now form some opinion as to the treatment of their own poor in particular. From their earliest days, the Quakers took this matter very seriously. In 1669, George Fox wrote to all Quarterly Meetings that they should make inquiry amongst poor Quakers with a view to apprenticing any children of such, one or two a quarter, to

[1] Gouge: *op. cit.,* pp. 114-124.
[2] Baxter: *The Christian Directory, Works,* VI, pp. 481f.
[3] Firmin: *op. cit.,* p. 39.
[4] Bellers: *An Essay . . . Improvement of Physick,* p. 20.
[5] Tyerman: *Life and Times of . . . Wesley,* I, pp. 422f; Myles: *A Chronological History . . . Methodists,* p. 21.
[6] *Journal,* III, p. 273 and p. 301; Warner: *op. cit.,* pp. 222f.
[7] Buer: *Health, Wealth, and Population in the Early Days of the Industrial Revolution,* p. 136. The Baptists, by the end of the eighteenth century, had 'friendly societies' for the relief and visitation of the sick in many places. A penny a week subscription was paid. There were also 'benefit societies' of a more modern sort. The poorer men paid a shilling a month, while others gave larger subscriptions, in order that all might be saved from distress in hard times—Carlile: *The Story of the English Baptists,* p. 172.

other Quakers, the Meeting to pay what was necessary. This would both relieve distress and ensure that Quaker children were brought up as Quakers.[1] A year previously, the Horsham Monthly Meeting recorded that one Bryan Wilkinson was loaned £5, and £5 each half year to be further loaned to him. John Shaw and Wm. Garton were requested to advance these half-yearly payments, but if the Quarterly Men's Meeting should decline to reimburse these two, then certain Friends undertook to provide the money.[2]

The Quaker Women's Meetings were often concerned as to the needs of those Friends who were poor. The Nottinghamshire Women's Quarterly Meeting started in 1671, and amongst its general instructions was one requiring that ' such as are poore or weake or wants Imployment to be looked after and relieved.'[3] The Minute Book of the Women's Quarterly Meeting for Cornwall, 1688-1734, shows the care of these women Quakers for the poor and sick.[4] The Bristol Minutes, 1694, record that one Rebecca Russell, who had been left by her husband, and who was destitute with four children, requested a loan of £20 from the Women's Meeting, stating that she could earn her livelihood ' by baking cakes and selling ayle.'[5]

There were Quakers in the early period who, being large employers of labour, were in a position to help. In Plymouth, for instance, serge makers kept over 500 poor people at work, and in Suffolk, a Friend employed more than 200 in woollen manufacture.[6] This relief of poverty within their own body was the most important social activity of the Quakers in the seventeenth century. They did not want their members to apply to the parish, while in the administration of this relief they were greatly helped by their intimate knowledge of, and discipline over, one another.[7] On the other hand, they took pains to prevent any one coming unnecessarily on relief. Their general principle was to encourage their poor to help themselves. As early as 1696, the Bristol Friends had established a workhouse, while the London Quakers five years later took

[1] *Journal of George Fox,* III, pp. 119f.
[2] *F.H.S.,* IV, p. 163.   [3] *ibid,* V, p. 138.   [4] *ibid,* IV, p. 32.
[5] Barclay: *The Inner Life of the Religious Societies,* p. 518.
[6] Braithwaite: *The Second Period of Quakerism,* p. 562.
[7] An illustration is found in *F.H.S.,* III, p. 59.

over a workhouse at Clerkenwell, which had been erected for certain London parishes in 1663. The Bristol venture, which was the more successful, had aimed from the beginning at relieving the able-bodied poor.[1] An illustration of this principle of assisting their poor members to help themselves is afforded by the Minutes of the Monthly Meeting of the County of Tipperary, under date the twenty-third, sixth month, 1696. A member named James Russell had fallen on evil times, and in order to assist him ' Friends were willing to lend him some cows and the said cows to be marked with a particular mark of some one of the meeting . . . and made over to Joshua Fennell and Samuel Cooke by bill of sale and board.'[2] Ten cows were lent Russell in this fashion.

Before the end of the seventeenth century the Quakers, within their own body, had devised the 'means test' in its most drastic form. In 1698, the Penketh Monthly Meeting decided that all persons who were a pecuniary charge to the Meeting must resign all their property to the Friends before receiving further benefit. This developed, so that by 1710 a complete Poor Law was framed by the Yearly Meeting, including a Law of Settlement.[3] 'No poor person receiving relief was allowed to remove without the consent of the Meeting, and a certificate to the Meeting where they were about to remove. Provided this Meeting received money from them for the use of the church, or " put them into any service of the church," it was " deemed a settlement," and if they behaved themselves " according to Truth " and were not chargeable for three years, they were also to be " deemed to belong to the meeting within the compass of which they shall inhabit." " Servant men and maids," after one year's faithful and honest service, were to be deemed to *belong* to the meeting to which they removed. In default of the regular papers being produced by a necessitous member, which, if he acted contrary to the advice of his meeting, they might refuse to give, the meeting *to* which he had removed has a claim to be reimbursed by the meeting *from* which he had removed,

[1] Isabel Grubb: *Quakerism and Industry before Eighteen Hundred,* p. 140.
[2] *F.H.S.*, 1918, p. 80.
[3] Barclay: *The Inner Life of the Religious Societies of the Commonwealth,* p. 519.

unless he had been "denyed" by this church.' This latter provision soon proved very onerous, and so the next year it was decided that the Meeting to which the person concerned had previously belonged should be required to reimburse only half the charges, the person being desired to return at the cost of his former meeting, on which his maintenance would then fall. For the purpose of this poor law, in 1721 the Yearly Meeting defined a member as one who 'was not denyed by his Monthly Meeting.' Sixteen years later, this poor law was codified in ten sections, which included a clause by which the Meeting into which the poor person removed, might claim for his relief from any Meeting where he had formerly resided, leaving such various Meetings to settle his last place of effective membership.

The next step in this development was also in 1737, when there was defined the 'Birthright Membership.' This stated that 'all Friends shall be deemed members of the Quarterly, Monthly, and Two-weeks Meeting, within the compass of which they inhabited or dwelt, the first day of the Fourth month, 1737 . . . the wife and *children* to be deemed of the Monthly Meeting of which the husband or father is a member, not only during his life, but after his decease.'[1] Not unnaturally, this valuable insurance element in Quaker membership led to corruption. To remedy this, the Friends excommunicated those whose lives were unsatisfactory ('disorderly walkers'); those who married out of the Society; and those who did not carefully observe the rules of the Church.[2] Positively, they sought to give a sound secular and religious education to every child who was considered to be a member of the Society. The introduction of poor persons into the membership of the Society tended to be discouraged, while the number of the poor previously in membership decreased.[3] By limiting membership to 'saints' and expelling 'sinners,' as the eighteenth century went on, the charity of the Friends was not so severely called upon. They

[1] Barclay: *The Inner Life of the Religious Societies of the Commonwealth*, p. 520. Also, Rufus Jones: *Later Periods of Quakerism*, p. 108; and, Society of Friends: *London Yearly Meeting During 250 Years*, pp. 35f.

[2] *F.H.S.*, 1923, p. 30—illustration of a Liskeard miner who, although a Quaker, was allowed at last to go to the workhouse because of his inveterate attendance at the public house. [3] Barclay: *op. cit.*, pp. 547f.

did not expel the poor as such, but a close investigation of character and life might reveal faults of which a more serious notice might be taken if the person concerned became poor. None the less, the Quakers succeeded in impressing others with their serious attempt to deal with the question of poverty within their own borders. They set out to have no Quaker apply to the Parish, and no Quaker in real want. In this apparently they succeeded.[1]

Nonconformists were early driven into the field of poor relief in a special way. Mention has already been made of their connexion with poverty through the sufferings of the ejected ministers. Most of these had little in the way of private means, and when it became apparent that the Act of Uniformity was going to stand, the Nonconformists set to work to relieve the wants of the ' new poor,' as they might not inaptly be called. To this end they had systematic lists drawn up by counties of all the ejected ministers, and had City and County committees elected, and treasurers appointed to receive gifts and distribute them to those necessitous ejected who could produce certificates of their sufferings. Some of the ejected ministers received help from wealthy or titled friends; many became Dissenting ministers; others schoolmasters; others reverted to their original trades; yet others emigrated; between thirty and forty became doctors; at least four became lawyers; about twenty obtained chaplaincies in hospitals or prisons. Yet there were many who were destitute except for the gifts they received, through what was really a Poor Fund. The income of the ejected ministers was often made up from more than one source, of which that of Oliver Heywood is an example. He stated that he received in regular contributions from his congregation about £5 per quarter; some occasional gifts, as for funeral sermons, baptisms, and other private services; and allowances from persons not belonging to the congregation, Lord Wharton and Lady Hewley being the chief.[2]

The General Baptists laid down certain rules for the treatment of their own poor as early as 1656, when ' Ye Gennarel Agrement of Ye Assembly of Messengers Elders and

---

[1] Eden: *The State of the Poor*, I, pp. 588f.
[2] Hunter: *The Rise of the Old Dissent*, p. 423.

Brethren' was drawn up. The question arose because some of their adherents had not scrupled to move from place to place 'deceivingly . . . requiring contributions in their own behalf.' It was accordingly laid down that when a member was in want, and the local congregation unable to relieve, the latter should send particulars of the case to other congregations, soliciting help, and all the time ' the person in want may follow his occasions and not bring himself in greater extremity by his going up and down neglecting his calling.' [1] Furthermore, in 1660, in ' A Brief confession or Declaration of Faith . . . ' they lay it down that the Deacons are to see that poor members want neither food nor clothing.[2] The 35th article, ' Of Communion of Saints, and giving to the Poor,' in the Confession of 1679, points out that members of the Church have a call on the charity of fellow-members, a real claim on the possessions of the more affluent, which claim, however, they lay down to stop short of anything in the nature of communism.[3] Individual churches acted on the same general principle as that laid down in these ' Confessions.' [4] The Baptists, regarding themselves as a body of men and women separated from the world and united in an exclusive church life, naturally felt a definite responsibility for the poor in their midst.

The existence of the original account book of the Stewards of the Methodist Societies of London for the period February 23, 1766, to December 31, 1803, indicates how much the London Methodists gave towards the poor.[5] Appendix VIII gives a summary for twenty years, 1770-1789, showing the income of each of the Societies, the sundries (which are not allocated to the different societies in the MS.), the expenditure on housekeeping, maintenance of preachers and their families, and the amount given to the poor. The receipts from the Bands and Classes (which sums are also included in the figures under the several societies) are separately given. It is not possible to say from this MS. how the money for the poor was distributed, nor who constituted the recipients, but

---

[1] *Baptist Minutes*, I, p. 8. [2] *ibid*, I, p. 17.
[3] McGlothlin, *op. cit.*, p. 151. [4] *C.H.S.*, I, p. 273.
[5] This important, but little-known, MS. is in excellent condition and is an unbroken record, although from 1792 the accounts are kept in a slightly different form, and are not quite complete.

it is a fair assumption that the poor of the societies would be the first to receive assistance and then other poor people.

It appears that the aggregate income of the Methodist societies in London during this period was :—

	Total Income	Receipts from Bands & Classes	Membership last year of each quinquenium
1770-1774	£11,113 8 6	3,030 13 8	2,452
1775-1779	10,711 10 11	3,120 15 0	2,436
1780-1784	14,010 15 6	2,990 15 1	2,680
1785-1789	13,478 0 5	2,788 8 2	2,680
1770-1789	49,313 15 4	11,930 11 11	

EXPENDITURE (ON CERTAIN ITEMS).

	Poor	Housekeeping	Preachers & Families
1770-1774	£3,707 0 9	1,604 12 1	1,273 17 7
1775-1779	4,034 19 4	1,926 12 0	1,219 5 0
1780-1784	3,923 9 4	1,284 8 0	1,238 13 0
1785-1789	3,333 19 5	1,169 16 11	1,528 1 0
1770-1789	14,999 8 10	5,985 9 0	5,259 16 7

From the above summary it appears that in twenty years the London Methodists gave away to the poor some £15,000. This is a remarkable figure when it is remembered that many of the members were poor and a considerable number were themselves receiving aid from this Poor Fund. Even more significant is the fact that many thousands of pounds were spent on buildings during this period, which money was raised mostly on loan, and not at the expense of the gifts to the poor. The only staple income of these Methodist Societies lay in the regular contributions of the Bands and Classes at the rate of 1d. per member per week, plus 1s. per member per quarter. The figures for ' Housekeeping ' are given above because they represent part of the cost of the Methodist Preachers; the item ' Preachers and Families ' includes the quarterly allowances made to preachers and the allowances in respect of their wives and families, medical expenses and the like. It should be noted, however, that the preachers participating in this were not only those working in connexion with these London Societies. For years London acted as a sort of unofficial central fund for the partial payment of preachers, and we find that the cost of maintaining the Methodist ministry in London, plus part of the cost of maintaining preachers and their families in various parts of the land, is almost exactly seventy-five per cent. of the sum given to the poor, a figure little less than extraordinary, with which probably no figures of present-day Methodism could compare. The effect of this concern for the poor by the Methodists, backed as it was by personal service in visitation and sick relief, could hardly fail to exercise its effect on contemporary opinion.[1]

---

[1] Concern for the poor within Nonconformity was not, of course, confined to the Quaker and Methodist bodies, although they were the leaders in this. A representative illustration of what was done by the Congregationalists is supplied by the records of the 'Above Bar Church,' Southampton. This Church, between 1770 and 1789, distributed to the poor the following sums:

					£	s.	d.
1770-1774	...	...	...	...	38	5	0
1775-1779	...	...	...	...	44	12	6
1780-1784	...	...	...	...	35	8	6
1785-1789	...	...	...	...	34	19	0
					153	5	0

These sums came from the Sacramental collections. No doubt money was also given by individual members of the Church, and was received from legacies.

Chapter IX

NONCONFORMITY AND PRESSING SOCIAL PROBLEMS

In the last chapter we have seen something of the reaction of Nonconformity to the great social problem of the eighteenth century, that of poverty. There were in addition certain other social problems of considerable magnitude. It is true that the anxious concern of modern times with this type of question did not exist in our period when people were hardly aware of a 'social problem' as such. They were, however, uncomfortably aware of the presence of certain 'sores' in the social body, of which three appear to the writer to come next in importance to the great problem of poverty. These three 'sores' were the liquor traffic and smuggling; the prison system; and slavery, and about them much has been written. It remains for us to notice the remarkable part played by Nonconformists in effecting changes in respect of each.

LIQUOR TRAFFIC AND SMUGGLING

As the principal articles smuggled were spirits, these two problems may conveniently be taken together. Contemporary literary references to the magnitude and evil effects of the huge liquor consumption of the period are numerous. While no statistics on this subject within this period can be accepted with confidence, because of the varying prevalence of illicit distilling and smuggling, it is possible from official sources to obtain figures which indicate the trend of consumption.[1]

---

[1] *First Report of Commissioners of Inland Revenue*, 1857, Appendix 19. The returns commence in 1684 and are given annually. On the also large consumption of beer, see Webb: *The History of Liquor Licensing in England*, p. 18; and *Econ. Hist. Supplt. to Econ. Journal*, May 1927, pp. 271f.

10

Year.	Spirits distilled. galls.	Year.	Spirits distilled. galls.
1684	527,492	1744	6,627,494
1694	810,096	1754	5,051,002
1704	1,375,496	1764	2,219,731
1714	1,950,827	1774	2,009,994
1724	3,563,625	1784	1,337,912
1734	6,074,562	1794	4,594,793

The rise of spirit drinking was not only a social phenomenon; it was also a political and economic question of some
importance. Prior to 1688, the supply of spirits came from
home production, confined to Royal patentees, and from im-
ports, chiefly French. In 1688, war broke out with France
and the importation of spirits was stopped. Two years later
the monopoly ended, and permission was given to all persons
who wished, to distil on payment of a low excise duty. As
a retailer of spirits did not require a licence, dram shops
rapidly increased, spirits became very cheap, and all classes
drank them. A series of Acts followed,[1] many of which were
ineffective, but before the end of the eighteenth century the
retail sale of all intoxicating liquors, for consumption on the
premises, was brought under the control of the justices, while
the policy, maintained ever since, of revenue duties on the
manufacture of spirits was adopted.

Although the volume of drinking remained high, and the
mortality due to it excessive, especially that resulting from
gin,[2] yet as the eighteenth century wore on, there were
influences which ultimately led to a considerable diminution.
As the evil of this excess became clearer and more undeniable,
the number of those who wished to see it curtailed grew.
Further, as the economic position of the working classes
tended to become worse towards the latter part of the century,
they were unable to spend so much in this way as previously.
But a new and very powerful factor appeared in the Evangelical Revival.

The Dissenters do not seem to have had a great deal to

[1] Report: *Royal Commission on Licensing (England and Wales)*, 1929-
31, pp. 264-269.
[2] Piette: *La Réaction de John Wesley dans l'Evolution du Pro-
testantisme*, p. 171, 'Les Médecins londoniens publièrent des statistiques
signalant les milliers de maladies incurables dues au gin: 14,000 cas
en 1750.'

do with the diminution of spirit drinking,[1] and it was amongst the Methodists that the chief Nonconformist opposition to the liquor consumption and trade developed.   This might be expected because by that time the problem had come to stand out against a background of social wretchedness; because many of the Methodist converts were from the ranks of those whose past environment had not supplied any effective check to over-indulgence; and because of the character and outlook of Wesley himself.   Wesley set his face against traffic in spirituous liquors, as well as against their consumption   His general view is indicated in one of his sermons: ' Neither may we gain by hurting our neighbour *in his body.*   Therefore we may not sell anything which tends to impair health. Such is, eminently . . . spirituous liquors . . . all who sell them . . . to any that will buy are poisoners general.' [2]   The application of the Golden Rule prevents engaging in the liquor trade.   Consumption is ruled out on similar grounds, and because of the physical harm which, Wesley held, must follow. Writing to Richard Steel in 1769, he urged: ' Touch no dram.   It is liquid fire.   It is a sure though slow poison.   It saps the very springs of life.' [3]   Wesley, writing on admission to membership of his famous societies, spoke of the requirement: ' First, by doing no harm, by avoiding evil . . . especially . . . drunkenness, buying or selling spirituous liquors, or drinking them, unless in cases of extreme necessity.' [4]   It became more and more difficult for a Methodist to have anything to do with the traffic in spirits.   It was made clear to the individual that the needs of his own soul demanded his abstention, while within the Societies a social conscience on this matter developed.   Nor was Methodist influence on this subject without its effect on the governing class in the period 1786 and afterwards,[5] when a movement inaugurated by the Anglican parson, Zouche, and the Evangelical philanthropist, Wilberforce, extended rapidly, being endorsed by the King and supported by the magistrates.

Smuggling was a considerable feature of eighteenth-century life because so many people were either employed in it, or

---

[1] For cases of discipline in this respect, see *supra,* pp. 62f, 65.
[2] *Sermons,* II, pp. 317f.   [3] *Letters,* V, p. 134.   [4] *Works,* VIII, p. 260.
[5] Report: *Royal Commission on Licensing,* p. 268.

profited by it.   It was a constant source of difficulty to successive Governments, and seemed at one time to present an almost insoluble problem.   For its successful continuance, smuggling depends upon the presence of at least three factors. There must be high duties on some articles for which there is a big demand; an inadequate preventive service; and a favourable public opinion.   These were all present in the eighteenth century.   A considerable proportion of the population was likely to have a direct interest in the continuance of smuggling as it was principally gin, the drink of the poorer section, that was introduced into the country in this way, although the consumption of gin was not confined to the working classes.[1]   Accordingly, any agency that could touch the poorer classes on this matter is likely to be important here.

While uncustomed goods were brought into the country at many points round the coast, there were certain particularly black areas, notably the Isle of Man, and Cornwall.   The prevalence of smuggling varied chiefly with changes in the rate of duties, and in periods when these were high, the serious nature of the problem is shown by the size of the rewards offered for the apprehension of smugglers.   £500 was not too large a sum to offer.[2]   Another serious aspect of this traffic lay in the corruption of excise men which sometimes occurred.[3] Fortescue, the Army historian, states that in Great Britain, the chief peacetime duty of the Army consisted in the protection of revenue officers and the reinforcement of the preventive service.[4]   This view receives corroboration from contemporary memoirs.[5]

The Quaker attitude condemned smuggling and any attempt at profiting by it as morally wrong on general principles, and also as offending against commercial integrity.   It was, however, in Methodism that the most effective opposition on the

---

[1] *Hist. MSS. Com. Tenth Report*, Part VI, p. 5.   Beresford: *The Diary of a Country Parson*: *The Rev. James Beresford, 1758-1781*, ' 1778, Feb. 23.   To my smuggler Andrews for a Tub of Gin . . . £1 5s. 0d.' ' 1780, May 17.   I did not go to bed until after twelve at night, as I expected Richard Andrews the honest smuggler with some Gin.'
[2] *Gentleman's Magazine*, 1747, pp. 152 and 398.
[3] *ibid*, 1774, p. 39.
[4] Fortescue: *A History of the British Army*, III, p. 8.
[5] *Lord Hervey's Memoirs*, II, p. 134, quoted George; *English Social Life in the Eighteenth Century*, p. 35.

part of any Nonconformist body to this traffic appeared.   In Cornwall and on the North-Eastern Coast, Methodism was taking firm hold, and in both those areas, smuggling was rife. Wesley attacked it fiercely and perseveringly.   He endeavoured to persuade people by his speech and writings to abandon the profits of smuggling, while he also made it a matter of energetic Church discipline.   Thus from the very beginning of Methodism, smuggling was banned by the same discipline which forbade the consumption of, or traffic in, spirits.

In 1767, Wesley wrote *A Word to a Smuggler*.   This was rapidly sold by thousands, and had a considerable effect amongst those actually engaged in the traffic.   The author would not allow an excuse of ignorance.   To the plea that one might not be able to tell if the goods offered for sale were smuggled or not, he demanded, ' Did not he that sold it tell you it was?   If he sold it under the common price, he did. The naming the price was telling you, This is run.' [1]   In this pamphlet, Wesley answered the question, ' Why should people not engage in smuggling? '   Because, he said, ' Open smuggling (such as was common a few years ago, on the southern coasts especially) is robbing on the highway. . . . Private smuggling is just the same with picking of pockets. . . . It is in effect not only robbing the King . . . but robbing every honest man in the nation.   For the more the King's duties are diminished, the more the taxes must be increased.' [2]   Wesley constantly insisted that the Methodist discipline should be sternly employed against any members of society who were in any way a party to smuggling.[3]   He saw to it that *A Word to a Smuggler* should be distributed right and left. Where the spiritual life of the Societies was strong, smuggling decreased.   Where smuggling was rife, there could be little spiritual vitality.   Such was Wesley's experience, and is in itself sufficient to account for his uncompromising hostility to the traffic.   ' I rode to Dover,' he recorded in December, 1765, ' and found a little company more united than they have been for many years.   Whilst several of them continued to rob the King we seemed to be ploughing upon the sand; but since they have cut off the right hand, the word of God sinks deep

[1] *Works*, XI, p. 170.   [2] *ibid*, XI, p. 167.
[3] See *supra*, pp. 66f.

into their hearts.'[1]   Year after year, the struggle against this trade went on, but not always with the success noted at Dover. In December, 1773, Wesley was in Sussex, in the Rye district, and found 'They do many things gladly; but they will not part with the accursed thing, smuggling.   So I fear with regard to these our labour will be vain.'[2]

For a century, the Government struggled with this traffic; for nearly half a century Wesley fought it within his societies. He finally won his battle before the statesmen won theirs, and this gradual extirpation of smuggling from the Methodist Societies was in itself a considerable contribution to the creation of a public conscience in the matter.   Dealing in uncustomed goods was a practice so widespread and so commonly condoned, that the presence of a body, constantly growing in numbers and influence, which at length would have none of it, can hardly have been other than influential. The very fierceness and duration of the fight Wesley had to wage within the societies on this problem is a measure of the importance of his final contribution to its solution. Gradually, he got preachers and people to hold his views in this matter, where formerly many of them had not.

THE PRISONS

The prison as we understand it had not come into existence in our period, the places in which people were then incarcerated being quite unlike modern prisons either in construction, control, or organization.   In the sixteenth, seventeenth and eighteenth centuries, there appear to have been in the country some 200 common gaols, as distinct from Houses of Correction.   These gaols were the property, and under the control, of a variety of authorities, the County Sheriff being responsible only for the county gaol.   Most of the municipal corporations had their own, while many liberties, franchises, and parts of counties had separate gaols.[3] In addition, a number of private gaols still existed, the property of Bishops, as at Durham, or of manorial lords, as in the case of Lord Arundel's prison at Penzance.[4]   These

---

[1] *Journal*, V, p. 151.   [2] *ibid*, VI, p. 6.
[3] Webb: *Prisons under Local Government*, pp. 2-5.
[4] Howard: *The State of the Prisons in England and Wales*, pp. 21 and 354.

common gaols were, in theory, places of detention, not of punishment, and were rarely specially constructed for the purpose. Such a gaol might be part of an old castle, or tower, or consist of dungeon-like rooms under a court-house or other public building, or even a few rooms in a public-house, as at Reading. Nor were they always secure.[1] Still more remarkable, from the modern standpoint, was the fact that the gaol was the private profit-making concern of its gaoler or owner, and consequently it was rare for the gaoler to be paid any salary. He lived by fees extracted from prisoners and by the profits of the sale of liquor and food. 'His sole obligation was to prevent the prisoners from escaping. This was the legal excuse for chains and irons.'[2] It is not remarkable that, with some exceptions, only a low type of man was to be found willing to take on the office of gaoler, nor is it difficult to understand why the condition of the prisons of the period was so very bad, seeing that it was against the interest of the gaoler to improve them, as improvements would cost money and to that extent reduce profits. The prisoners had to keep themselves. Sometimes their usually meagre resources were supplemented by private charity, and in some cases by the 'county bread.' This term covers a dole, in money or food, given out of the county funds for the maintenance of convicted felons, which dole even did not always reach them in full.

The Bridewells, or Houses of Correction, were nominally administered by the Justices. Originally they existed in order to deal with people who were disorderly, or who would not work, but who could be placed in a bridewell and compulsorily set to work. It was during the seventeenth century that they lost this poor-law character, and had become places where minor offenders could be punished. Early in the eighteenth century, it became difficult in practice to distinguish between a House of Correction and a common gaol. In administration or the lack of it; in discipline and conduct; in the character of, and effects upon, the inmates, the two different institutions had closely approximated. Without methods of extortion, it was difficult to make a profit out of these gaols, hence torture

---

[1] *C.S.P.D.*, Jan. 2, 1662/3, gives illustration of this insecurity.
[2] Webb: *op. cit.*, p. 9.

of one sort and another was employed, while on the other hand, 'benefits' could be purchased, especially such as had to do with drunkenness and vice. In some cases the gaolers ran brothels as a side line to their business, but it was the encouragement of drunkenness that was the more serious.

The beginning of our period, 1660-1800, saw the Nonconformists suffering a long and intimate acquaintance with the prisons, while the end of this period saw a movement for prison reform in progress, which, though by no means the sole work of Nonconformists, yet owed much to some of them. While Nonconformists of different persuasions, such as the Baptist John Bunyan,[1] suffered in prison for their beliefs, it was the Quakers who were those chiefly affected. For the greater part of the latter half of the seventeenth century they formed a not inconsiderable part of the population of the gaols, in some cases overcrowding them. The Quaker record of Sufferings shows that between 1650 and 1689, 367 deaths of Friends in prison are known to have occurred.[2] Quakers naturally became active in the work of prison reform and visitation during the next century. We find Bellers petitioning the City of London to provide more prison accommodation so as to prevent overcrowding, with its probable consequence of disease. Like other Quakers, he did not sentimentalize over the needs of those incarcerated. He wanted sanitary conditions and strict regulation. In 1699 he wrote, 'the Gaols want regulating: for whilst the keepers are allowed to sell strong liquors it provokes their prisoners to great expense, and they often live high, to be more in the Gaolers' favour.'[3] Firmin, somewhat similarly, denounced the relative luxury that was possible in many prisons for those who had the means to pay for it.[4]

The Methodists had a real interest in prisoners. Primarily, they were anxious about their souls, but they were not entirely forgetful about their bodies. Both of the Wesleys and

---

[1] Bunyan: *A Relation of the Imprisonment of Mr. John Bunyan* . . . *written by himself*, pp. 243f.

[2] Graham: *William Penn*, p. 172. Also, Besse: *op. cit.*

[3] Bellers: *Essays about the Poor, Manufactures, Trade, Plantations, and Immorality*, p. 19; *An Essay Towards the Improvement of Physick*, p. 30; *An Epistle to Friends . . . concerning the Prisoners, and sick, in the prisons. . . .*

[4] Firmin: *op. cit.*, pp. 41 and 44.

Whitefield visited prisons frequently.   John Wesley started
this work in 1730, and at various times in his diary records
his impressions while visiting and preaching in different
prisons.[1]   Amongst the prisons he visited were Newgate,
London; Newgate, Bristol; Castle and Bocardo, Oxford;
Exeter; York; Carrickfergus; Whitley.   The needs of the
prisoners were not overlooked in the hymns published for the
Methodist Societies.[2]

One of the most remarkable effects of Methodism on prison
life concerns the Bristol Newgate and its gaoler, Dagge.[3]   He
was converted under the preaching of George Whitefield in
1737[4] and in the course of the next twenty years that prison
was completely changed, the Annual Register of 1761
recording its approval of what had been done.[5]   Wesley,
describing the actual changes, indicated by contrast what had
been the previous state.   Writing in 1760, he said that cleanliness was now everywhere, fighting and brawling put down,
any prisoner wronging another being punished.   Drunkenness
and whoredom were quite stopped, while idleness was prevented as far as possible.   ' Those who are willing to work at
their callings are provided with tools and materials, partly by
the keeper who gives them credit at a moderate profit, partly
by the alms occasionally given, which are divided with the
utmost impartiality.   Accordingly at this time, a shoemaker,
a tailor, a brazier, and a coach-maker are all employed.'
Religious and medical services were provided, and now ' the
whole prison had a new face.   Nothing offends either the eye
or ear, and the whole has the appearance of a quiet, serious
family.'[6]   The work of this gaoler, Dagge, was the outcome
of his religious experiences, and is of great importance.   A

---

[1] *Journal*, IV, p. 52, and VII, p. 41.
[2] *Hymns of Intercession for all Mankind* (1758), No. 27; *Hymns and
Sacred Poems by Charles Wesley* (1749), Vol. I, No. 100.   One of the
most remarkable works done in a prison by a Methodist was that of
Silas Told, begun in 1744 as the result of a profound conviction gained
during a sermon of Wesley's.   He began regular prison visitation and
continued it for thirty years—*An Account of the Life and Dealings of
God with Silas Told, late preacher of the Gospel, written by himself*,
p. 78.   Many of the early Methodist preachers were visitants at different
prisons—*Preachers*, II, pp. 71 and 175f; V, p. 30.
[3] Samuel Johnson: *Lives of the English Poets (Life of Savage)*,
II, pp. 423f and 429.
[4] Simon: *The Revival of Religion in England in the Eighteenth Century*, pp. 202f.   [5] *Annual Register*, 1761, p. 61.   [6] *Journal*, IV, pp. 416f.

comparison of what he had already accomplished compared with what Howard later advocated, shows that this prison, with which Howard was certainly familiar, had to a not inconsiderable extent anticipated by some fifteen years the reforms for which the latter was to press.

John Howard, the most famous name in the annals of prison reform in this country, came from the ranks of the Nonconformists.[1] His account of the prisons as they were is noteworthy for its restrained recital of facts, and for the exact way in which he recorded all the relevant data.[2] As a reformer, he was no advocate of luxury in prisons, nor was he a sentimental critic. He wanted cleanliness and humanity, under strictly observed regulations. He advocated considerable alteration in the structure of prisons, and the removal of some of their terrible hardships, but denied that the effect of these changes would be to diminish the deterrent effect of the prison regime.[3] His principal proposals concerned health, segregation, discipline, and work. In regard to health, Howard urged that gaols should be built where air and water were abundant, that a fumigator for infected clothing should be provided; every room should be lime-washed twice a year, and swept and cleaned daily; the prisoners should be kept clean, and have clean clothes; the bread allowance ought to be by weight and not price, and some other food should also be provided; each gaol ought to have its own surgeon or apothecary, and an infirmary should be available.[4] Concerning segregation, the reformer argued that each criminal should sleep alone; women kept separate from men, and young criminals from old; debtors and felons should be totally separate, and bridewells distinct from gaols.[5] In regard to discipline, Howard wanted the gaolers to be carefully chosen, to be salaried, and to have no liquor licences; proper discipline to be maintained, and inspections by

---

[1] Howard's father was a keen, virile Independent, a man who had made a considerable sum of money in business as an upholsterer—*C.H.S.*, IX, p. 255.

[2] The story of how Howard, having been pricked as Sheriff of Bedfordshire, visited the county gaol, and then made his famous tours, at home and abroad, of inspection of prisons of all kinds, is well known, and needs no repetition here.

[3] Howard: *The State of the Prisons in England and Wales*, p. 51.

[4] *ibid*, pp. 26, 29, 36-38, and 40.

[5] *ibid*, pp. 27-29.

specially appointed unsalaried inspectors, to be frequently carried out.[1] He argued in favour of a workshop for debtors, and believed also that work should be done in bridewells, during stated hours, as a part contribution towards the expenses, although he realized the product of such involuntary labour could not be sufficient to make the bridewell a paying concern. All profit obtained from work done outside the stated hours should go to the worker, while Howard thought it might be worth while also to give the worker a percentage of the profit for the work done in stated hours. 'With regular economy, prisoners would be better nourished, and fitter for labour, than they now are; and yet the county not burthened with much, if any, additional expense. But a building fit for the intention ought first to be provided.'[2] Howard urged that prisoners should be subject to no fees, and so would remove at once one of the chief abuses of the contemporary prison system.[3]

It is difficult to determine with accuracy the result of Howard's revelations and advocacy, as a good deal of the effect would be indirect. By the year 1789, however, he was able to enumerate some forty-two new gaols or Houses of Correction as under construction, although some of them took years to complete.[4] In the field of legislation, some results appeared early. In 1774, two Acts were passed, the first concerning the health of prisoners, and the second ordering that prisoners acquitted or discharged, should be released in open court, and no discharge fees should be levied upon them.[5] Five years later, Blackstone and Eden worked out an elaborate code of prison discipline, which had its effect on the legislation of the next dozen years.[6]

If Howard's direct influence on the county prisons left much reformatory work to be done, his influence on the gaols and Houses of Correction not under the County Justices was considerably less. 'The Municipal Corporations and private owners of prisons largely disregarded both Howard's revela-

---

[1] Howard: *The State of the Prisons in England and Wales*, pp. 31f, 41, and 43.   [2] *ibid*, pp. 30, and 48f.   [3] *ibid*, p. 36.
[4] Webb, *op. cit.*, p. 51.   [5] *ibid.*, p. 38; cf. Howard, *op. cit.*, p. 21.
[6] Webb, *op. cit.*, p. 38; *The Reading Mercury and Oxford Gazette*, May 8, 1786, No. 1268, records verbatim the new Rules and Regulations adopted by Berkshire Quarter Sessions, for the better government of the County Gaol, illustrating the new attitude.

tions and the relevant Acts of Parliament.'[1]   The irresponsibility and variety of the English prison system made the way of reform difficult, and the reforms when they did appear were the work of several different strains, religious, humanitarian, legal, and political, of which that supplied by the Evangelicals was not the least important.

SLAVERY

The long fight for the abolition of slavery did not, of course, attain success until the nineteenth century, but the change in public opinion which finally made this success certain was principally due to factors which belong to our period. Amongst these factors, Nonconformist opinion and activity was important. We may start with the views of Baxter who, in a fairly long discussion,[2] did not pronounce categorically against slavery, nor did he altogether condemn white slave labour. He argued that a white might rightfully be enslaved, either voluntarily by selling himself on account of poverty, or legally when slavery was imposed in lieu of death, no wrong being done since the lesser punishment was inflicted instead of the greater.[3]   Captives, apparently irrespective of colour,

[1] Webb: *op. cit.*, p. 63.

[2] Baxter: *The Christian Directory, Works,* IV, pp. 212-220.

[3] This idea was not uncommon at the time, and Baxter's thought here may be reminiscent of Petty, who in *A Treatise of Taxes . . . Ireland,* p. 68, said, 'Why should not insolvent thieves be rather punished with slavery than death?' Similarly, Locke, *Two Treatises of Civil Government,* p. 128, '(A man) having by his fault forfeited his own life by some act that deserves death, he to whom he had forfeited it may, when he has him in his power, delay to take it, and make use of him to his own service; and he does him no injury by it. For, whenever he finds the hardship of his slavery outweigh the value of his life, it is in his power, by resisting the will of his master, to draw on himself the death he desires.' This, Locke called 'the perfect condition of slavery,' and would admit the validity of no other. White slavery, in fact, was quite common in the seventeenth and in part of the eighteenth century. In theory, it was indentured or penal labour, but it really formed a branch of the slave trade. 'Malignants' of the Civil Wars and men who had engaged in rebellion at some time, were amongst those thus enslaved in the West Indies—see *Hist. MSS. Com. Eighth Report,* Part I, p. 514, and *Var. Coll.,* Vol. V, p. 176, for contemporary accounts. Further, this form of slavery had some connexion with negro slavery on economic grounds for as the African Slave Trade developed, it became unprofitable, owing to the costs of transportation, to ship English felons to the plantations. The consequent problem of the disposal of these felons was solved by the method of paying contractors so much a head, usually five pounds, to dispose of these convicts in North America. Nor was this method abolished until the nineteenth century. Usually over a third of those transported died en route, while the remainder were auctioned by the ordinary slave-auctioneers—see Lecky: *op. cit.,* VII, pp. 325f.

taken in a lawful war might sometimes be enslaved, according to Baxter.   His general principle was that slavery, as such, was not to be condemned, provided that it neither wronged God nor injured the Commonwealth, nor endangered the salvation of the individual concerned.   Accordingly, it followed that in the case of slavery by contract or consent, the slave must have time for Divine worship and be ' exhorted and kept from sin ' ; and he must not be denied such comforts as are needful to his cheerful and grateful service of God.

Baxter argued that negro slavery was indefensible except on such grounds as apply to whites.   He said : ' To go as pirates and catch up poor negroes . . . that never forfeited life or liberty . . . is one of the worst kinds of thievery in the world.'   The chief end of the slave-owner must be the conversion of the slave, and a truly converted slave must be freed, as indeed the law required.   The owner should make sure that the slave was not embracing Christianity merely as a means to the end of his freedom.   On the other hand, the owner must be on the watch lest his desire for the continuance of the slave's service should cause an abatement of his desire for his salvation.[1]   Baxter's teaching in this respect is interesting in that he was quite conscious that Christianity implies the brotherhood of man, but he drew the unusual conclusion that therefore whites, as well as blacks, might be enslaved.   He did not try to explain away slavery, but was genuinely convinced as to its rightfulness, and even desirability, in given circumstances and with adequate moral and spiritual safeguards.

The first anti-slave petition to Parliament, in the mid-seventeenth century, was the work of a Cambridge Baptist minister, and the petitioners condemned this form of labour both on religious and economic grounds.   ' Nor can your petitioners help observing with sorrow that a slave trade is a dishonour to humanity, a disgrace to our national character, utterly inconsistent with the sound policy of commercial states, and a perpetual scandal to the profession of Christianity.'[2] Throughout the eighteenth century, it continued to be debated, not only whether slavery was compatible with the Christian

[1] Baxter : *How to do Good to Many, Works*, XVII, p. 330.
[2] Quoted by Carlile : *The Story of the English Baptists*, p. 172.

religion, but whether it was economically sound, and even whether it was not an economic necessity for the cultivation of the West Indies.

Defoe both condemned the slave trade and contributed to the legend of the 'noble savage.' In *The Reformation of Manners* he denounced the trade, and in his *Life of Colonel Jacque*, he urged that negroes should be better treated, arguing that under more humane treatment, 'the negroes would do their work faithfully and cheerfully . . . they would be the same as their Christian servants, except that they would be the more thankful, and humble, and laborious of the two.'[1] In Man Friday, Defoe showed how a coloured man could be a devoted comrade, implying that negroes, and other savage races, were not by nature so utterly inferior, as some upholders of slavery alleged.

The earliest Nonconformist body to hold enlightened views on slavery was the Society of Friends. As early as 1671, George Fox, while on a visit to Barbadoes, exhorted Friends 'to cause their overseers to deal mildly and gently with their negroes, and not use cruelty towards them . . . and that after certain years of servitude, they would make them free.'[2] From this time on, Quakers were concerned with the question, and their views progressively developed. In 1727, the Society of Friends, at their Yearly Meeting in London, reached this conclusion : ' It is the sense of this Meeting that the importing, by Friends, of Negroes from their native country and relations, is not a commendable or allowed practice, and is, therefore censured by this meeting.'[3] This rather tepid resolution was the beginning of a series of actions spread over the next half-century, in which their attitude steadily hardened. All Quakers were warned against the slave trade in 1758 on the grounds that it involved a denial of the Golden Rule, and it ' furnisheth encouragement to those poor, ignorant people to perpetuate their savage wars in order to supply the demands of this most unnatural traffic, whereby great numbers of mankind, free by nature, are subjected to inextricable bondage . . .'[4] In 1761, and again in 1763, it was deter-

[1] Klingberg : *The Anti-Slavery Movement in England*, p. 31.
[2] George Fox : *Journal*, II, p. 149.
[3] Society of Friends : *Book of Christian Discipline*, p. 159.
[4] *ibid*, p. 159.

mined to exclude from the Society any who continued to be implicated in the trade. The Quakers gave up the slave trade prior to dealing with slavery itself; they acted first and evolved a coherent view afterwards. In Pennsylvania, as early as 1696, the German Quakers had advised against the slave trade. By 1754, they were calling the trade 'man-stealing,' and in 1774 and 1776, expulsion from the Society was decreed for all who had anything to do with the slave trade, or who would not emancipate their slaves. By 1780, 'there was not a single slave owned by any member of the Society, with its knowledge and consent in America or England.'[1]

Organized effort against slavery began in this period. In 1783, the Quakers petitioned Parliament. The following year they issued 12,000 copies of an anti-slave pamphlet,[2] and in 1785 circulated a book by Anthony Bezenet on the condition of the negro slaves in the British colonies. Bezenet was originally a French Huguenot, who came to London on the revocation of the Edict of Nantes, there joining the Quakers. He went to Philadelphia where he became a schoolmaster, and began a series of literary productions against slavery. The importance of this Quaker lies not only in his actual work against the institution of slavery, but also in the fact that he influenced two of the most important figures who stood against this trade—Clarkson and Wesley. Clarkson, while still a student at Cambridge, was greatly stirred by a book of Bezenet,[3] while the same book, or another by the same author,[4] led Wesley to join the anti-slavery movement. The Abolition Society began in 1787, formed of nine Quakers, Clarkson, Granville Sharp, and one other, Wilberforce acting as chief adviser. There was a long fight in Parliament during the next five years, until the outbreak of the French Wars absorbed the attention of Parliament, and it was not until 1833 that all British slaves were by law emancipated.

[1] Barclay: *The Inner Life of the Religious Societies of the Commonwealth*, p. 554.

[2] *The Case of Our Fellow-creatures, the oppressed Africans, respectfully recommended to the serious consideration of the Legislature of Great Britain, by the people called Quakers*, see Klingberg: *op. cit.*, p. 66.

[3] *An Historical Account of Guinea, its produce, and the general disposition of its inhabitants, with an inquiry into . . . the slave trade, its nature and calamitous effects.*

[4] *Caution and Warning to Great Britain and her Colonies on the calamitous state of the enslaved Negroes.*

Turning to the Methodists, we find an apologist for slavery in George Whitefield, who nevertheless fought hard for the betterment of the actual condition of the slaves. At times, even he seemed to have doubts as to the rightfulness of slavery,[1] but in 1748 he tried to influence the Georgia trustees to introduce slavery into that colony.[2]   When some three years later it was introduced, he was delighted, advancing three arguments in favour of it, namely, that slavery provided an opportunity for saving the souls of the ' poor Ethiopians ' ; that slavery was an institution present in, and uncondemned by, the Bible; and that, in any case, it was necessary as hot countries could not be cultivated without negroes.   It was in Georgia, too, that the concern of the Wesleys with slavery developed.   John Wesley was one of those who had opposed the introduction of slaves into that colony, and he denounced the traffic in white slaves.   In 1774, he wrote to the *Monthly Review* inveighing against the inhumanity of American slave-owners,[3] and in the same year he published ' Thoughts upon Slavery,'[4] a dozen years before the foundation of the ' Society for the Suppression of the Slave Trade.'   This pamphlet reveals considerable knowledge of the history and geography of slavery, slave-transportation, and slave-law.   In addition to the religious, moral, and philanthropic arguments, the writer dealt with the economic argument of the necessity of slavery for the cultivation of hot countries.   Wesley denied this alleged necessity, arguing that white men, including Englishmen, were quite well able to labour in hot climates, provided that in food and drink they were temperate, and that they inured themselves by degrees to labour under these conditions.   He backed this argument by an appeal to his own experience in Georgia.[5]

[1] George Whitefield : *Works*, IV, pp. 37ff.
[2] It had not previously been allowed because the Trustees wanted to encourage an industrious type of settler, for which they knew it was vain to hope if slave labour were employed.
[3] *Works*, XI, pp. 56ff.   [4] *Letters*, VI, p. 126.
[5] Methodism followed Wesley's lead.   Many gave up the use of sugar because it was 'a drug composed of the slave dealer's sin and the slave's misery'—Blanshard : *op. cit.*, p. 140.   The Wesleyan Conference of 1791 decided to procure signatures to an anti-slavery petition, and 229,426 names were forwarded while twenty-one other nonconforming bodies, including Roman Catholics, secured only 122,978—quoted from *Wesley Studies*, p. 190, by Maldwyn Edwards, *John Wesley and the Eighteenth Century*, p. 124.

The part played by Nonconformity in the anti-slave crusade was important. Nonconformists were early in pronouncing against it; one of their sections was the first to free itself from any complicity in it; their influence in the Abolition movement was large. Nevertheless, it was not until towards the end of our period that they reached a considerable unanimity on this question. The ultimate success of the Abolition movement, as far as it was accomplished by altruistic forces, depended upon the work of two main groups —those whose interest in the slaves was not primarily religious, and those for whom the religious motive was paramount. In some ways, Defoe may be regarded as a link between them. The former group comprises the humanitarians who on general principles wanted to alleviate the lot of the slaves, and the natural philosophers who believed in the existence of the noble savage, and who assisted in combatting the charge that the African natives were a lower type of humanity for whom slavery was not only fitting, but desirable. The second group included the Quakers, the Evangelicals, the Methodists and other Nonconformists. The Quakers were first in the field, and their support of the Abolition Movement was very powerful. The Evangelicals included Wilberforce as their chief representative on behalf of the slaves. The importance of the Methodists, in addition to the advocacy of Wesley himself, lay in the influence of Methodist missionaries and adherents in the late eighteenth and early nineteenth centuries, and in their influence on the growth of the Evangelical party in the Church of England. The other Dissenters do not show up largely in this connexion, perhaps because they had not at this time a membership on both sides of the Atlantic so active as was that of either the Quaker or the Methodist bodies.

We have now briefly reviewed three of the important social problems of the period 1660-1800. In respect of the first of these, Liquor and Smuggling, we have discovered that the branch of Nonconformity specially concerned took an uncompromising line, anticipating effectively in its own ranks what State action only succeeded in accomplishing on a nation-wide scale later. Regarding the second, Prisons, it was the work of a Nonconformist that was of outstanding

11

importance. In the case of the third, Slavery, it was a Nonconformist body that supplied the principal force for the reformers. Is this connexion between Nonconformity and social progress accidental or significant?

That their religion had a vital bearing upon these men's activities cannot be doubted. Their passion for reform was not the unaided product of humanitarianism. It is true that, in the case of Howard, the humanitarian element was important; it was not, however, exclusive. His interest in prisons began because his religious sense of duty, imbibed from his Independent upbringing, compelled him fully to carry out his functions as sheriff, although a full discharge of those duties was unique at the time. Nor can it be said that Evangelicalism as such was the cause of this social work: some of these men were evangelicals and some not. The significance of the Nonconformist influence in social reform in the eighteenth century must be sought in their history. Nonconformists could not forget the persecutions which their fathers and grandfathers had suffered, not only because they were near them in time, but because they still laboured under legal disabilities, often irksome, while more and more the new blood coming into their body was from the poorer strata of society. They saw social problems, therefore, not in the mass, but as they were presented in the lives of individuals; they had with them a personal touch. This direct concern supplied a dynamic which was rendered more effective because of the reality of their Church discipline.

CHAPTER X

CONCLUSION:

THE NONCONFORMIST CONTRIBUTION TO SOCIAL AND ECONOMIC LIFE, 1660-1800

RELIGION affects, and is affected by, the everyday life of a people. During times of religious stagnation the force of this interaction is lessened, and the religious life of the majority of Church adherents tends to be restricted to a separate compartment of life. But every religious revival tends to break down the walls of this compartment and to flood all life's activities with religious aims and sanctions. Hence to study any period of intense religious activity is likely to involve the study of social and economic change. At the same time, care must be taken lest those social and economic changes which are observed should be attributed unduly to religious causes. A general summary of this study, in which an attempt has been made to avoid a one-sided view, may now be attempted.

During our period, the principal religious activity in this country was amongst the Nonconformists. This activity had important effects on the social and economic life of the country. That such should be the case is not surprising seeing that this period of Nonconformist history formed an important arch in the bridge connecting the medieval attempt of the canon law to control economic activities, and the laissez faire of the nineteenth century. It also connected chronologically a social life based on an agricultural system with one based on industry.

The Nonconformists, as a whole, do not appear to have had one coherent social theory. Their concern was primarily, although by no means exclusively, with the individual soul, but the insistence which most of them placed upon right conduct led them out from a merely personal and individual conception of religion, since conduct involves a reference to others. Not only were some branches of Nonconformity more awakened socially than others, but the degree of sensitiveness to the claims of social life on the part of any particular denomination sometimes varied considerably within our period; further, one denomination might be very concerned with one social problem, whilst almost oblivious of another. Nonconformists did not take up an entirely new attitude on social questions. On the contrary, they accepted ideas common in their day and in preceding periods, although they modified these, consciously or otherwise. Thus, the old view of society as functional was one from which Nonconformity did not disentangle itself in our period, but social function was interpreted in a more inward way. As the chief concern of man was the salvation of his soul, his social and economic position must be kept subservient to that end. Similarly, Nonconformists tended to modify the static conception of society because of their understanding of the doctrines of stewardship and vocation. A man might be born into the labouring section of the community and might have it pointed out to him how fortunate was his position in that he was not exposed to the temptations which are liable to accompany the possession of wealth, but it was not difficult to believe that it was God who was calling him to a higher status if he showed unusual abilities. Again, the strict view of the importance of not wasting time, and even of the duty of gaining wealth, characteristic of certain of the denominations in particular, militated against the permanence of a static view of society. This was of no little importance as the Industrial Revolution, with its need for mobility of labour, both geographically and between groups, was drawing near. On the other hand, amongst the principal Nonconformist bodies, there was a tacit acceptance of the maintenance of class distinctions. Thus, although Baxter and Wesley both denounced prodigal expenditure on the part of the rich, Baxter recognized that the poor should not expect, apart from the question of cost, to dress like the rich, while Wesley accepted the idea that men of money should leave their children in such a position as to enable them to preserve the standard of living to which they had been accustomed.

Religious dogmas, firmly held, affect social outlook and social practice. This is particularly noticeable in the seventeenth-century Quaker and the eighteenth-century Methodist. The Quakers' belief in the Inner Light, and in the essential equality of man, caused them to be distinguished socially from others in a marked way; indeed, their refusal to pay the conventional respects would alone separate them. Similarly, the hold which the Methodists had on the doctrines of Original Sin, Christian Perfection, and Scriptural Holiness, gave a definite form to their social as well as to their individual life. They were sure that natural man is a wholly evil creature, but one nevertheless capable of Christian perfection.[1] So the individual is bidden, in all his activities and interests, to seek a certain quality of life, which involved almost always a radical change.[2] Nor does this concern each individual alone, for it is the task of every Methodist, as it was the sole task of every Methodist itinerant, to spread Scriptural Holiness throughout the land. It is not enough to flee from the wrath to come; others must be assisted urgently to the same end.

It has always been difficult to apply Christian principles to economic practice; indeed, from time to time Christian teachers have appeared who have regarded wealth as a thing evil in itself, necessary perhaps, but none the less evil. The great leaders of Nonconformity did not take this attitude but, on the contrary, tried to grapple with the situation brought about by the breakdown of traditional views. In periods of notable religious activity, the economic order is apt to be subject to criticism from the ethical point of view, and it is not therefore surprising to find in our period men whose religious feeling and belief was strong, tilting at the current facts and views of economic life. It was a critical and difficult time. In the centuries before, the Medieval Church had sought to assert its supremacy over the State and to solve social and economic problems on religious and ecclesiastical lines. In the nineteenth century, economic activity was, with a large measure of success, to assert its right to pursue its

[1] *Sermons,* II, pp. 211-222 and 150-174.
[2] *ibid,* II, p. 225. 'Know your disease! Know your cure! Ye were born in sin : therefore, "ye must be born again," born of God. By nature ye are wholly corrupted : by grace ye shall be wholly renewed.' *ibid,* II, p. 169. Wesley argues, from Scripture, that there are several stages in Christian life, of which the highest is that of Christian Perfection—'*A Christian is so far perfect, as not to commit sin.*'

own way irrespective of Church control or teaching. Puritanism, coming chronologically between the two, was in accord with neither.[1] Among the Protestants two views developed, the latter of which tended to oust the former. Some conceived of a Christian Order in social and economic matters while others regarded the sphere of the Church as limited to personal life and not directly concerned with social affairs. Like that of Calvin, the attitude of English Puritanism towards private property and the acquisition of wealth was not one of opposition. It was held that the institution of private property had a Divine sanction, seeing that part of the divinely promulgated Decalogue presupposed the existence of private property, while the Bible contained many examples of the serious nature of theft, and the sinfulness of theft implies the rightfulness of property. Wealth as a necessary means for the service of the community might be used to the glory of God. Accordingly, wealth and private property constituted no problem in itself; the problem consisted in the definition of the limits within which it might be obtained, and the methods by which it might be increased.[2]

[1] cf. Tawney: *op. cit.*, pp. 102ff. Seventeenth-century English Puritanism had Calvin in the background. Calvin broke with the Canon Law doctrine of usury, perceiving that a lender performs an economic service, and that interest is not in itself evil. None the less, he was suspicious of interest, which, he held, should have an official maximum rate. Loans ought to be no one's sole business; both borrower and lender should be able to benefit, and the latter is entitled to a moderate rate of interest. This is not laissez faire; neither is it traditional Church ethics. In some ways, the attitude towards interest provides a significant division between the older Canon view and the newer Calvinistic or Puritan. These two views of economic life, however, probably have as much in common as otherwise.

[2] cf. Troeltsch: *op. cit.*, II, p. 600. Although there was a Puritan spirit discernible in the Anglican Church the present writer claims that this spirit was far more generally at home in the Nonconformist bodies, and that in fact the latter were heirs to that spirit and tradition. Contemporaneous popular expressions of the Puritan outlook amongst Anglicans are to be found in *The Whole Duty of Man* (1658) and in *The New Whole Duty of Man* (which by 1780 had reached its twenty-fifth edition). Much of what these works have to say about economic relationships does not differ materially from the writings of Nonconformists divines, but usually lacks something of the pointedness and vigour of the latter. What is, however, much more important is that the landed interest maintained its close attachment to the Anglican Church, while the mercantile classes were closely allied to the Nonconformists. Therefore the views of the Nonconformists on business morality are necessarily of much more importance than those of Anglicans seeing that from the practical point of view the latter were not so much concerned.

Distinguished authorities have given an opinion, often quoted by others, that England was saved from revolution in the eighteenth century, and in the period following, by the Methodist Revival.[1] It is true that Wesley's enormous personal influence, and the influence of the societies owing their origin to him, was on the side of King and Government, and was therefore anti-revolutionary. The fierce opposition and persecution the Methodists received in the mid-eighteenth century, often connived at or worse by the magistrates themselves, might have encouraged them to disloyalty, and even insurrection. In fact, it did neither. But the writer is unable to find proof of the view that Methodism prevented a revolution. It is true at times great unrest prevailed and that Methodism taught loyalty as part of its religion, but so did the other Nonconformist bodies, who had hardly yet begun to be affected by the Revival, and so did the Church of England. The truth would rather seem to be that while there were factors favouring an upheaval—the Jacobites, the disturbances consequent upon the American War, the high price of food and the economic distress of 1756-7 and later after 1770,[2] and some sympathy with the French Revolution —there were also a number of factors working in the opposite direction. Amongst these were, the loyalty taught on religious grounds to some extent by all or almost all the religious bodies; the memory of past political upheavals; and the general disinclination of the English people to revolt. The Methodist influence was real and important; it was not so great that without it a revolution would have broken out.

The principal contribution of Nonconformity to social and economic life is to be found in what it did for individual

[1] Halévy: *op. cit.,* Book III, p. 339. 'We shall witness Methodism bring under its influence first the dissenting sects, then the establishment, finally secular opinion . . . we shall explain by this movement the extraordinary stability which English Society was destined to enjoy throughout a period of revolutions and crises; what we may truly term the miracle of modern England, anarchist but orderly, practical and businesslike, but religious and even pietist.' *The Cambridge Modern History,* VIII, p. 764. 'Dissenters of other kinds were inclined to favour the Revolution; from the first Wesleyans met it with rigid hostility—an attitude of which it is difficult to exaggerate the national importance. The teaching of the one man who had really stirred the masses in the middle of the century went all towards allaying their excitement at its close.'

[2] Wadsworth and Mann: *The Cotton Trade and Industrial Lancashire,* pp. 356-9.

members.   As we have seen, its wealthy and influential
adherents, of whom there were many in the seventeenth
century, gradually disappeared, and their place was taken by
people who became later wealthy and influential, but people of
obscure Nonconformist origins.   Those who rose to affluence
in the Industrial Revolution had diverse religious origins,
while the personal life of others was uninfluenced by any of
the religious bodies.   But these men mostly belong to the
nineteenth century, whereas we find during the eighteenth
century many Nonconformists rising notably in the world—
Wesley, indeed, regarded the Devil as interested in this
phenomenon.[1]   Is there anything in Nonconformist teaching
or Church life to account, at least in part, for this rise towards
affluence? The answer must be that there is.   We have seen
that some Nonconformists, particularly Quakers and Methodists, inculcated a doctrine of personal responsibility which
resulted naturally, and almost inevitably, in the encouragement
of the economic virtues of thrift, industry, prudence, fore-
sight, and energy.   Also, since unnecessary expenditure and
speculation were frowned upon, profits could be, and very
often were, put back into businesses.   And we find that, on
the one hand, Nonconformists looked after their own poor,
sometimes with a striking carefulness; while, on the other,
they helped poor people, as no one else did, to rise above
poverty.   This is important and has been noticed by various
writers.   What was also important and is rarely noticed, is
the fact that the Nonconformist Church organization was of
such a character as would often encourage the emergence into
social activity and significance of classes of people who for
the most part might otherwise have remained inarticulate:
the poor, and women.   During our period, the important
period leading up to, and embracing the first part of, the
Industrial Revolution, it may be said that the Nonconformist
Churches provided the only large-scale opportunity of a
systematic sort for the development of powers of initiative
and responsibility amongst the proletariat.   This opportunity
was not, it is true, equally characteristic of all the Nonconformist bodies.   The Presbyterians were far more 'clerical'
than the other denominations, and the place given to the laity

[1] See *supra*, p. 94.

was, in fact, very largely reserved for the more important members. With the Independents and Congregationalists, however, it was different. Each local, ' gathered,' Church was autonomous. In some of the large early Independent Churches the personal power of the minister was very great, but usually within their body the laymen had more opportunity than within the Presbyterian. Amongst the early Dissenters it was the Baptists who offered an exceptional scope and encouragement to laymen of low social and economic position. They met in Assembly composed of Messengers (sometimes called Angels), Elders and Brethren. As they had no separated ministry, great opportunity was offered to the ordinary member. Their power of survival and expansion, already noted, may probably be taken as evidence of their importance in providing social training and developing individual initiative amongst the poorer classes. The organization of the Quakers in ' meetings,' monthly, annual, and so on was highly democratic.[1] They provided a valuable social training for types of independent, self-reliant, and yet considerate persons, who could be concerned for the social and economic needs of men outside their own body. From the first, women took part in their affairs on the same footing as men, and thus had opportunities, denied them almost everywhere else at the time, of personal initiative and combined action.[2] The real difference between them and other women of the seventeenth and eighteenth centuries lay, not in their characteristic garb, nor in any other external factor, but in individual self-reliance and initiative. Margaret Fell, the wife of George Fox, was the first of a long line of such women.

From the social point of view the Methodist organization had contradictory elements which later, chiefly in the nineteenth century, caused considerable disruption. The authority of Conference was final and complete over the whole organization, and that Conference was not, in its earlier stages, elective, being in fact a method of expressing the will of Wesley himself. On the other hand, in the local

[1] The Yearly Meeting, held in London, to which representatives from various parts of the country came, dates from 1672.

[2] As in the distinctively ' Women's Meetings,' see *supra*, p. 138.

societies, the organization was such as was calculated to develop both initiative and a strong social sense. From 1738, the organization of the devout, i.e. those who were seeking Christian Perfection, into Bands or Select Bands, was in operation. These Bands usually comprised between five and ten members, and met weekly. Men, women, married, and unmarried persons met in separate Bands. In turn they told of their temptations and their spiritual victories and experience. All they could spare towards a common stock they were expected to bring in, while expulsions from membership were subject to their consent. In 1742, the institution of the Class Meeting began, each class consisting of twelve or more. These class meetings often formed the nuclei of new societies to which any desiring ' to flee from the wrath to come and to be saved from their sins' might come. The class-leader knew each member and dealt with the spiritual and moral condition of each in turn, also interesting himself in their temporal concerns. The usual contribution expected from each member was a penny a week and a shilling a quarter.[1] Thus were ordinary, and not infrequently illiterate people, trained to self-expression; given moral and social as well as spiritual standards; and made to feel their solidarity with those like-minded. In some instances, the leaders of these Classes would be men of very humble status. The wage-earner who was the leader of a Band or Class would in that capacity exercise what might be a very real power over those of a higher economic or social position. Women in Methodism had opportunities given them second only to those given to female Friends. As preachers and as leaders of local societies these women exercised a real influence. Wesley took several women as well as men with him on some of his preaching tours. He accepted the doctrine of the Priesthood of all Believers, nor did he refuse its logical conclusion, that women are therefore equal with men in spiritual work. 'God owns women in the conversion of sinners, and who am I that I should withstand God?'[2]

---

[1] N.H.M., I, p. 288.

[2] ibid, I, p. 322. Amongst early Methodist women preachers were Grace Murray, who travelled with Wesley himself, off and on, for some ten years; Mary Bosanquet, afterwards the wife of Fletcher of Madeley; Sarah Crosby, who itinerated over a wide area having Leeds as centre,

Women were freely admitted to the chief local courts of spiritual and financial affairs, the Leaders' and Quarterly Meetings.

There are two other important contributions made by the Nonconformists, qua Nonconformists, which must be noted. First, in the sphere of political freedom. The struggle for political freedom in this country was not only fought on the battlefields of the Civil War and in Parliament, it was also in part fought by those whose prime concern was for religious liberty. It is no doubt possible to have a considerable measure of religious liberty under an otherwise tyrannical rule, but in fact religious and political liberty are usually related. It is significant, too, that a charge of sedition was constantly being brought, throughout our period, against one or other of the branches of Nonconformity. Between 1660 and 1672, there was some excuse for this charge, afterwards little or none. But the way in which the charge came up again and again shows that in the mind of the authorities and others a desire for religious freedom spelt a movement for political change, and that the attainment of the one meant the progress of the other. Moreover, we have found that some, notably the Unitarians, whose fight for religious freedom was still going on when that of the Dissenters (in the more limited sense of the term) had already been almost completely won, were definitely out for an increased measure of political liberty.

The contribution of the Nonconformists in the field of education must be noted.[1] This arose out of the religious needs and disabilities of the early Dissenters, for Nonconformists naturally looked askance at the usual channels of

[1] Important though its social effects were, the Nonconformist contribution to education has not been dealt with in this book because there are already several books dealing at length with this—see Bibliography.

and who 'during one year . . . travelled nine hundred and sixty miles, held one hundred and twenty public services, led six hundred class and private meetings'; Miss Mallett, who worked in Suffolk and Norfolk and who was granted authority by the 1787 Conference as a preacher 'as long as she preaches the Methodist doctrine and attends to our discipline'; Ann Cutler, of the Bradford district; Hester Ann Rogers, wife of one of the itinerants; and others. The Independents, in a lesser degree, also provided opportunities for women. 'Every member of the congregation (i.e. Independent), whether male or female, had a voice or vote . . . in all the concerns of the church'—Toulmin: *An Historical View of the State of the Protestant Dissenters*, p. 280.

education, seeing these were in the hands of the State Church. In 1660, all Nonconformist schools were made illegal and remained so until the Toleration Act, upon which a large number were opened. A further advance followed the judges' decision in 1700, that the bishops' courts had no jurisdiction beyond the grammar schools, while the year following saw a ruling that no elementary schools required a licence. Even in periods of persecution the Nonconformists continued to keep their own schools, another illustration of how their fight for a full religious freedom involved a fight for other sorts of freedom. Although there were early cases of Nonconformist elementary and secondary schools, it is in the field of higher education that their contribution was really valuable. The Nonconformists were, as such, shut out from the old Universities, so they made possible a higher education for their sons by means of their Academies, the period of which is almost co-terminous with the period of our investigation. These Academies were of different sorts, some existing primarily for the theological education of intending ministers, others not being primarily theological. The earlier were often run by ejected ministers, and some were not localized, i.e. they went wherever the ex-minister, usually under threat of persecution, moved. The influence of these Academies was totally out of proportion to their number or size. At a time when the standard of university education and examination had become deplorable, they provided a wide curriculum and a high standard of teaching. Indeed many Anglicans sent their sons to them.[1] But we are concerned here especially with social and economic effects, to which these Academies made a not unimportant contribution. Some of them, and some of the Nonconformist secondary schools, offered an education more suitable to the sons of merchants and others engaged in business life, than could otherwise be obtained at the time. Nonconformist schools were pioneers in technical education.

Mention should also be made of the pioneer educational work amongst the masses done by Wesley. He perceived

---

[1] Those who were, or who soon became, Anglicans, and were educated at one or other of these Academies, included Archbishop Secker, Bishops Butler and Jacobsen, and Bowes the Lord Chancellor of Ireland.

that ignorance and the Christian religion, if not actually incompatible, were inimical to one another. Accordingly, he set out, first to create an appetite for knowledge, and then to satisfy it. His contribution to popular education was simply conceived. He did not set out to organize anything in the nature of adult classes, but sought to get books into the homes of the people. So he himself produced the *Christian Library*, partly consisting of books written by himself, but more usually of other works which he abridged.[1] The *Christian Library* was the forerunner of the cheap popular 'libraries' of to-day. It was not enough for a man of Wesley's mind to create a desire for reading and to supply the means for its satisfaction, he must ensure that the books supplied were effectively distributed. Accordingly, not content with putting them on the market in the usual way, he sent them round by his preachers, whose saddle-bags almost always had their load of literature for sale. Thus Wesley's cheap publications found their way into thousands of humble homes. Indeed, evangelical conversion itself often had as a sequel the overcoming of illiteracy in the individual. Men who were converted frequently set to work to learn to read so that they might be able to read the Bible. Moreover, they not only read it, they saturated themselves in it, a liberal education in itself.[2]

In spite of different origins and notwithstanding a certain amount of rivalry between themselves, the different Nonconformist bodies developed a similarity of outlook. This was partly the result of inward constraint and partly of outward circumstances. The former because they were in a real measure the heirs of the Puritans; the latter because of active persecution and, enduring long after it, legal disabilities. The result was the existence of a large body of people with a common attitude towards social and economic conditions, at a time when those changes which have so transformed modern England, were already plainly appearing.

---

[1] He published *A Short English Grammar* in 1748, at the price of 1d., and the year before, *Primitive Physick*, which went through twenty-three editions during his lifetime. He also put out short Latin, French, Greek, and Hebrew Grammars, a *Complete English Dictionary* in 1753, and a *Concise History of England*, in 4 vols., in 1776, and many other works.

[2] Nonconformists took an active part in the popular elementary education given by the Sunday schools in the period post-1780. Methodism led the way in the voluntary character of the teaching given.

APPENDIX I

DISSENTERS' PLACES OF WORSHIP
REGISTERED UNDER THE TOLERATION ACT, 1689[1]

Period.		England. Tem-porary.	Per-manent.		Wales. Tem-porary.	Per-manent.		QUAKERS. England & Wales. Tem-porary.	Per-manent.
1688-1690	...	796	143	...	—	—	...	131	108
1691-1700	...	1247	32	...	—	—	...	80	6
1701-1710	...	1216	41	...	3	—	...	98	3
1711-1720	...	862	21	...	13	—	...	46	1
1721-1730	...	439	27	...	9	—	...	30	3
1731-1740	...	418	21	...	6	3	...	82	3
1741-1750	...	495	24	...	7	3	...	74	1
1751-1760	...	693	54	...	10	1	...	27	5
1761-1770	...	691	71	...	10	14	...	20	5
1771-1780	...	965	142	...	13	16	...	10	3
1781-1790	...	1135	280	...	19	36	...	10	2
1791-1800	...	3218	768	...	261	147	...	12	11

[1] *Parliamentary Papers,* 1852-53, pp. 78, 79, and 82.

These figures are given in the official Returns by Counties and Denominations. In the case of the latter, little value can be attached to them because by far the largest items are those headed respectively, ' Protestant and Protestant Dissenters,' and ' Denomination not specified,' i.e. too indefinite. The separate figures for the Quakers are, however, given above because it seems less likely that they would be returned under either of the two general classifications just mentioned. They are probably the only denominational figures in the Return to which much reliance can be attached. Many of the 'Temporary' Places of Worship would be private houses, barns and the like, where a religious service could be held in a room or building, ordinarily serving some quite different purpose.

APPENDIX II

COMPARISON, BY COUNTIES, OF CONGREGATIONS (OR PASTORAL CHARGES) OF DISSENTERS IN ENGLAND, IN 1715 AND 1773

County.	1715 Total No. of Congregations. E.	N.	Hearers.	Baptists Only. E.	N.	1773 Total No. of Congregations.	Baptists only.
Bedfordshire	18	23	4760	14	22	19	15
Berkshire	20	26	4920	7	10	14	5
Buckinghamshire ...	14	17	a. 2290	5	7	25	15
Cambridgeshire ...	21	23	5140	4	5	19	7
Cheshire	23	21	8295	3	3	24	3
Cornwall	14	12	1190	2	—	8	3
Cumberland	14	19	2249	—	2	16	2
Derbyshire	27	28	—	—	—	27	1
Devonshire	75	61	24105	7	6	58	16
Dorsetshire	28	35	—	4	5	25	2
Durham	6	9	1270	—	—	15	3
Essex	45	52	13866	7	8	50	13
Gloucestershire ...	40	51	8389	14	16	49	26
Hampshire	35	32	a. 7341	12	9	28	8
Herefordshire ...	9	8	1680	1	1	9	4
Hertfordshire ...	24	26	6360	12	10	18	8
Huntingdonshire ...	7	13	1440	1	1	13	5
Kent	42	52	—	18	27	46	30
Lancashire	46	47	18319	1	4	61	14
Leicestershire ...	28	33	5665	9	9	36	9
Lincolnshire ...	10	22	1762	—	3	23	17
Middlesex	86	91	—	23	26	68	13
(including part London—see next page)							
Monmouthshire ...	14	8	3391	7	2	13	6
Norfolk	19	20	—	3	4	22	9
Northamptonshire ...	41	40	8810	22	22	37	16
Northumberland ...	25	27	7720	—	—	40	3
Nottinghamshire ...	18	8	4247	1	1	17	9
Oxfordshire	15	14	3400	6	3	11	3
Rutlandshire ...	3	6	510	1	3	5	3
Shropshire	16	15	2017	2	2	11	3
Somersetshire ...	66	55	a. 19110	13	12	50	13
Staffordshire ...	15	16	4560	1	2	14	—
Suffolk	40	34	a. 9700	5	—	31	3
Surrey	36	20	—	11	4	13	2
(including part London—see next page)							
Sussex	30	16	4031	8	1	19	12
Warwickshire ...	19	18	—	5	4	21	7
Westmorland ...	5	5	521	—	—	3	—
Wiltshire	31	20	8070	7	4	38	19
Worcestershire ...	17	18	3460	8	8	15	6
Yorkshire	62	48	a. 12343	—	—	69	21
ENGLAND ...	1104	1089	210931	244	246	1080	354

E = Calculation based on the Evans List.
N = Calculation based on the Neal List.
a. = Figures for some Churches in this County omitted in the MS.
N.B.—The figures for the Hearers are from the Evans List, and the number of Hearers is given when all, or nearly all, the churches in the County have their figures recorded. In a few cases, two sets of figures are shown in the MS. for the Hearers, supplied by different persons. In such cases the lesser figure is usually given here.

Thompson, in his MS. (1773), inserts the following comment on the figures for London, which are supplied below :—
' Those (Churches) marked as not in the approved list are such eccentric irregular Preachers and Societies as are in no Connexion with either of the Denominations. Some are a reproach to any religious profession, many of them from a factious turbulent spirit, have broken off from the churches they were in communion with, and but few of them do much credit to Christianity.'

				LONDON	
				1715	1773
Recognized :—					
Presbyterian	...	...	...	28	19
Congregational	...	...	...	21	18
Baptist	...	...	...	25	13
				74	50
Irregular :—					
Presbyterian	...	...	...	–	4
Congregational	...	...	...	–	5
Baptist	...	...	...	–	8
Unspecified	...	...	...	2	–
				2	17
Total	...	...	...	...	76	67

London here includes the Cities of London and Westminster, and the Borough of Southwark. The rest within the Bills of Mortality are given in their respective counties.

APPENDIX III

COMPARISON, BY COUNTIES, OF CONGREGATIONS (OR PASTORAL CHARGES) OF DISSENTERS IN WALES, IN 1715 AND 1773

County.	Total No. of Congregations. E.		Hearers.	Baptists Only. E.	N.	Total No. of Congregations.	Baptists only.
		N.				1773	
Brecknockshire ...	6	3	1770	1	2	10	2
Caernarvonshire ...	1	2	250	—	—	2	—
Cardiganshire ...	7	3	a. 2700	—	—	15	1
Carmarthenshire ...	11	9	b. 4100	1	4	31	4
Denbighshire ...	3	3	440	1	2	4	2
Flintshire	1	1	25	—	—	1	—
Glamorganshire ...	12	7	c. 3606	5	4	24	4
Merionethshire ...	1	1	150	—	—	2	—
Montgomeryshire ...	4	2	420	—	—	5	—
Pembrokeshire ...	6	8	d. 1400	3	—	?	?
Radnorshire	6	4	2150	2	3	8	3
WALES	58	43	17011	13	15	102	16

(Monmouth figures are included under England.)

Notes on the above figures for Wales :—

1. It would be unsafe to draw any detailed conclusions from these figures because the information given is far less complete or clear, than in the case of the English counties.

2. It is often difficult to decide, when two or more places are bracketed together, if they are to be counted as one or more.

3. In the case of Pembrokeshire, the names of six men, and of six towns are given, with no other information. Perhaps there were unorganized churches meeting in private houses.

4. Anglesey figures are included in Caernarvonshire.

5. The congregations were more numerous than the above figures suggest (which are really figures of Pastoral Charges), as not infrequently two or more places are grouped together, usually served by one minister. Such cases are included as one congregation, as apparently they comprise one central church with subsidiary causes.

a. = 2,700 hearers in 6 churches, no figures given for remaining church.
b. = 4,100 „ 10 „ „ „ „
c. = 3,606 „ 7 „ „ „ 5 churches.
d. = 1,400 „ 2 „ „ „ 4 „
E = Calculation based on the Evans List.
N = Calculation based on the Neal List.

13

APPENDIX IV

STATISTICS OF
EIGHTEENTH-CENTURY METHODISM[1]

Year.			Circuits.			Members.
1765	...	...	39	...	...	—
6	...	...	40	...	...	19,753[2]
7	...	...	41	...	...	25,911
8	...	...	40	...	...	27,341
9	...	...	46	...	...	28,263
1770	...	...	49	...	...	29,496
1	...	...	47	...	...	31,022
2	...	...	47	...	...	31,484
3	...	...	47	...	...	32,274
4	...	...	49	...	...	33,468
5	...	...	50	...	...	34,997
6	...	...	55	...	...	36,678
7	...	...	58	...	...	38,274
8	...	...	60	...	...	40,089
9	...	...	62	...	...	42,486
1780	...	...	64	...	...	43,830
1	...	...	63	...	...	44,461
2	...	...	66	...	...	45,723
3	...	...	69	...	...	45,995
4	...	...	73	...	...	49,169
5	...	...	76	...	...	52,431
6	...	...	85	...	...	58,156
7	...	...	94	...	...	62,088
8	...	...	99	...	...	66,375
9	...	...	99[3]	...	...	70,305
1790	...	...	108	...	...	71,463
1	...	...	115	...	...	72,476
2	...	...	121	...	...	75,278
3	...	...	131	...	...	74,925
4	...	...	137	...	...	83,368
5	...	...	138	...	...	90,347
6	...	...	143	...	...	95,906
7	...	...	145	...	...	99,519
8	...	...	149	...	...	101,712
9	...	...	156	...	...	107,802
1800	...	...	161	...	...	109,961

[1] Compiled from the *Minutes of the Methodist Conferences, from the First, held in London, by the late Rev. John Wesley, A.M., in the year 1744,* the 1812 and 1862 editions, the latter edition having various alterations and additions.

[2] Incomplete, no figures being given for London, Canterbury, Norwich, Oxfordshire, Devonshire, Dunbar, Wales, or Ireland.

[3] The total of Circuits should be larger, as those in Ireland are omitted for this year, but the figure for membership is apparently complete.

APPENDIX V

THE WEALTH AND INFLUENCE OF NONCONFORMISTS IN 1715, AS SHOWN BY THE EVANS MS.

(ENGLAND)

County.	Gentlemen.	Tradesmen.	Farmers & Yeomen.	Labourers.
Berkshire	a. 81	a. 242	a. 36	
(Also 3 Esq. Probably large number of substantial men.)				
Cheshire	237	441	709	619
(Probably many wealthy and substantial men.)				
Cornwall	51	109	55	184
Cumberland	61	a.	a.	a.
(One merchant at Whitehaven worth above £20,000; four more worth about £4,000 each.)				
Derbyshire				
(Probably many wealthy and substantial men.)				
Essex	273			
(Also 2 Esq.)				
Gloucestershire ...				
(Some colliers)				
Hampshire	24			
(13 wealthy, i.e. in addition to the 24 gentlemen; 375 substantial; 500 'middling'; 'mean' or poor, about 1,300.)				
Kent	41	22		
(Information given for three churches only.)				
Lincolnshire	72	a. 48	a. 2	a. 4
(1 Esq.)				
Monmouthshire ...	60	256	597	492
(3 Esq.)				
Northumberland ...				
(12 Esq. Many farmers and substantial farmers. One minister mentioned as getting £100 p.a. salary, possibly the Presbyterian minister at Riveley. Also stated that one member at North Shields raised 100 men in 'ye late rebellion.')				
Nottinghamshire ...	177	a. 155	a. 24	a. 26
(16 Esq., includes 9 widows of Esquires, and one Esquire's lady. Probably a lower percentage of poor than most counties.)				
Oxfordshire ...	a. 120	a.	a.	a.
Rutlandshire ...	21	53	15	28
Shropshire	21	137	150	
(1 Esq. Probably many yeomen and well-to-do farmers.)				
Somersetshire ...	20			
(For figures for Bristol, see pp. 51f. Figures given for few churches.)				
Surrey	a.			
('Persons of £500,' 102.)				

179

APPENDIX V

County.	Gentlemen.	Tradesmen.	Farmers & Yeomen.	Labourers.
Sussex	90	123	43	66
(15 ships' captains. Chichester, 22 men and women from £300-£100 p.a.)				
Westmorland	18			
Wiltshire	27	a. 76		
(1 Esq., 1 merchant, 'very rich gent.,' 4; 'Worth £500 or more,' 79. Dissenters quite wealthy in this county.)				
TOTAL	1,394 and Esq. 39	1,662	1,631	1,419

a. = Some, or many. When prefixed to a figure, means that the MS. indicates some, or many, in addition, to the actual number, if any, given.

Counties, the names of which are italicized, have full, or almost full, information for the churches in the MS.

Wiltshire—The 'Worth' is given of congregations as follows :—Westbury, £33,500 (800 hearers); Leigh, £30,650 (650 hearers); Warminster, 'Of estates sufficient for Justice of the Peace,' 4; 'their total value, £90,000.'

There is no information, or little, given as to the wealth and influence of Nonconformists in the MS. for the Counties not included above.

APPENDIX VI

THE WEALTH AND INFLUENCE OF NONCONFORMISTS IN 1715, AS SHOWN BY THE EVANS MS.

(WALES)

County.	Gentlemen.	Tradesmen.	Farmers & Yeomen.	Labourers.	Notes.
Anglesey					Included in Caernarvonshire.
Brecknockshire					No information given.
Caernarvonshire					1 Esq.
Cardiganshire					No information given.
Carmarthenshire					No information given.
Denbighshire	a. 34 (at Wrexham)	a.			No beggars. At D e n b i g h 'One worth between £4,000 and £5,000. 3 worth £500 each.
Flintshire					At Newmarket one worth between £1,400 and £1,500.
Glamorganshire	2	17	167	210	
Merionethshire					1 Esq.
Montgomeryshire	7				Freeholders, 6; many poor.
Pembrokeshire					No information given.
Radnorshire					No information given.
WALES ... and Esq.	9 2	51	167	210	

a. = Some, or many. When prefixed to a figure, means that the MS. indicates some, or many, in addition, to the actual number, if any, given.

APPENDIX VII

DISSENTERS HAVING VOTES IN 1715 (EVANS MS.)

ENGLAND.	Dissenters having votes for:—			Total.	Total Quaker Voters.
	County.	Borough.	Magistracy.		
Bedfordshire				776	
Berkshire	379	273		652	100
Buckinghamshire ...				190	
Cambridgeshire ...	263			263	
Cheshire	894	9	48	951	
Cornwall	58	67	12	137	
Cumberland	151	37		188	250
Derbyshire				6	
Devonshire	1118	1011	638	2767	
Dorsetshire				—	
Durham	22	30		52	24
Essex	1034	577	162	1773	
Gloucestershire ...	687		60	747	
Hampshire	481	3	157	641	27
Herefordshire ...	49	43		92	
Hertfordshire ...	557	220		777	132
Huntingdonshire ...				115	
Kent	191	148		339	
Lancashire	1328	237		1565	
Leicestershire ...				608	
Lincolnshire	148	34		182	
Middlesex	306	73	33	412	
Monmouthshire ...	337	183	170	690	
Norfolk				—	
Northamptonshire ...				986	
Northumberland ...	339	5		344	
Nottinghamshire (a)...	623		429	1052	
Oxfordshire	207	16	16	239	
Rutlandshire ...	26		34	60	
Shropshire	178	109		287	
Somersetshire ...	25	75		100	
Staffordshire	541	45		586	
Suffolk				111	
Surrey	66	89	44	199	
Sussex	330	219	168	717	
Warwickshire ...				—	
Westmorland	62	2		64	
Wiltshire	274	26	50	350	
Worcestershire ...				16	
Yorkshire	385	56		441	
	10436	3587	2021	19475	
	623				

DISSENTERS HAVING VOTES IN 1715 (EVANS MS.)

WALES.	Dissenters having votes for:— County.	Borough.	Magistracy.	Total.	Total Quaker Voters.
Brecknockshire ...				78	
Caernarvonshire ...	5	8		13	
Cardiganshire ...				56	
Carmarthenshire ...				108	
Denbighshire ...	60	21		81	
Flintshire	1	3		4	
Glamorganshire ...	209	130	115	454	
Merionethshire ...	12			12	
Montgomeryshire ...	11	11		22	
Pembrokeshire ...	30			30	
Radnorshire	102			102	
	430	173	115	960	

(a) The MS. does not state to which category this figure belongs.

As will be seen, only a few of the County Correspondents included Quakers on their return.

The following points should be borne in mind in studying the above table :—

1. Incomplete. There are no figures for some counties in the MS., while in the case of others, the figures for some towns are omitted.
2. It is doubtful in a number of cases, owing to illegibility, as to what the particular figure ought to be.
3. The many erasures and notes in the MS. suggest that wherever possible considerable care has been taken to get accurate figures.
4. Double Votes. Most probably there are numerous cases of this sort not reported. The few recorded are entered in this Appendix as single votes.
5. Dissenters influenced many voters not themselves Dissenters.
6. Voters under any given county may include some who lived in that county but who had votes in another county, or counties.
7. It is sometimes doubtful in which category of voter a given figure should be included.

APPENDIX VIII

EXTRACTS FROM THE CASH BOOK OF THE LONDON METHODIST SOCIETIES.

(Receipts)

(Year) Foundery or New Chapel.	West Street.	Spitalfields.	Snowsfields.	Wapping.	Westminster.	Sundries.	Total.
(1770) 786 11 0	502 17 7	164 2 10	86 11 3	19 11 5	31 6 0	678 11 6	2269 11 7
(1771) 772 15 8	491 14 10	181 0 8	89 7 2	23 5 9	22 9 6	591 4 2	2171 17 9
(1772) 789 11 4	525 14 11	191 16 5	84 6 9	21 2 0	30 10 10	692 15 9	2335 18 0
(1773) 810 6 7	535 13 10	203 8 5	100 12 11	17 12 9	25 2 7	502 18 10	2195 15 11
(1774) 786 9 3	494 4 8	174 9 8	88 14 2	31 19 5	17 15 8	546 12 5	2140 5 3
3945 13 10	2550 5 10	914 18 0	449 12 3	113 11 4	127 4 7	3012 2 8	11113 8 6
(1775) 870 12 2	522 19 1	182 2 5	80 11 3	34 9 11	20 18 11	428 9 6	2140 3 3
(1776) 823 5 5	496 5 1	204 11 8	95 4 6	32 17 8	19 4 1	503 0 11	2174 9 4
(1777) 810 10 7	538 5 11	222 1 1	73 0 1	37 7 11		434 9 6	2115 15 1
(1778) 803 9 8	566 1 5	204 5 4	82 19 4	29 17 8		485 15 9	2172 9 2
(1779) 811 10 6	536 0 7	51 1 1	100 12 4	35 3 6		574 6 1	2108 14 1
4119 8 4	2659 12 1	864 1 7	432 7 6	169 16 8	40 3 0	2426 1 9	10711 10 11

Foundery or (Year)	West Street	Spitalfields	Snowsfields	Wapping	Sundries	TOTAL
(1780) 728 14 7	503 1 3	92 7 3	103 18 8	64 18 7	582 12 10	2075 13 2
(1781) 1106 7 2	520 2 8	74 11 10	84 1 7	49 12 10	606 2 10	2440 18 11
(1782) 1046 14 6	479 0 11	75 2 2	88 17 2	45 11 10	1861 18 6	3597 5 1
(1783) 1114 11 3	477 10 2	77 8 8	90 1 3	39 16 9	1223 13 6	3023 1 7
(1784) 1053 0 4	478 13 9	78 16 5	83 11 6	39 9 5	1140 5 4	2873 16 9
5049 7 10	2458 8 9	398 6 4	450 10 2	239 9 5	5414 13 0	14010 15 6
(1785) 947 2 5	460 9 11	66 1 9	85 5 5	41 5 2	464 14 1	2064 18 9
(1786) 1161 4 5	474 4 2	68 8 6	85 18 0	51 0 0	1502 3 11	3342 19 0
(1787) 1047 19 8	571 16 6	64 7 0	87 13 8	69 12 9	784 0 5	2625 10 0
(1788) 1272 2 11	615 16 9	81 1 10	89 10 7	61 4 6	449 17 4	2569 13 11
(1789) 1275 19 2	598 9 7	66 14 5	96 15 8	72 6 1	764 13 10	2874 18 9
5704 8 7	2720 16 11	346 13 6	445 3 4	295 8 6	3965 9 7	13478 0 5

London Methodist Societies, 20 years' receipts, £49,313 15s. 4d.

The use of the Foundery ceased, and New Chapel, City Road, was opened in 1778. The figures in the first column after that date applying therefore to New Chapel, and not the Foundery.

There are no Receipts from the Westminster Society after 1776.

From 1781, the Burial Ground brings in a varying income.

'Sundries',—for 1784 includes £700 borrowed for New House; and £300 borrowed in 1789.

The usual items found on the Receipts side of these accounts are:—Seats; various collections; money from Classes and Bands; Rent; Poor-box. Of these, receipts from Bands and Poor-box are usually small.

The usual items under 'Sundries', include:—Visitation (usually the largest item); special and sundry gifts and collections; Kingswood School; subscriptions for chapel debt; sums borrowed, the figures for 1782 for instance, include large sums raised for the New Chapel Debt.

(EXPENDITURE, PART ONLY)

Year.	House-keeping.			Preachers & Families.			Poor.			Receipts from Bands & Classes.			Members, London.
1770	273	12	7	206	17	4	758	15	10	603	9	7	2292
1771	338	4	6	253	18	9	745	14	10	601	9	6	2420
1772	352	10	10	251	15	6	704	13	7	621	2	1	2441
1773	323	5	5	281	15	0	783	14	3	606	19	2	2442
1774	316	18	9	279	11	0	714	2	3	597	13	4	2452
	1604	12	1	1273	17	7	3707	0	9	3030	13	8	
1775	356	9	1	244	2	0	784	1	4	657	5	4	2492
1776	393	3	8	210	6	0	874	18	4	612	10	0	2425
1777	432	6	2	246	13	0	809	1	3	629	16	11	2512
1778	420	15	7	230	2	6	809	17	0	623	2	1	2559
1779	323	17	6	288	1	6	757	1	5	598	0	8	2436
	1926	12	0	1219	5	0	4034	19	4	3120	15	0	
1780	253	19	10	218	17	6	763	7	4	602	5	4	2498
1781	293	3	7	234	11	6	795	4	0	614	11	4	2511
1782	299	8	7	234	7	0	747	19	0	599	18	4	2515
1783	254	17	1	282	2	6	847	12	4	579	5	10	2617
1784	182	18	11	268	14	6	769	6	8	594	14	3	2680
	1284	8	0	1238	13	0	3923	9	4	2990	15	1	
1785	189	18	4	270	13	0	727	14	11	594	19	5	2437
1786	236	19	1	252	3	0	645	5	4	527	18	1	2517
1787	210	2	7	351	7	0	662	13	3	541	15	7	2600
1788	238	4	8	313	5	0	652	18	7	559	6	7	2800
1789	294	12	3	340	13	0	645	7	4	564	8	6	2680
	1169	16	11	1528	1	0	3333	19	5	2788	8	2	
1770-1789	5985	9	0	5259	16	7	14999	8	10	11930	11	11	

The Membership figures are taken from *Minutes of the Methodist Conferences* (1862 edition).

There are other expenses to do with the Houses which are not included in the Accounts under 'Housekeeping,' e.g. rent, repairs, candles, servants. If these were included, the total spent on the houses would be rather more than double the 'Housekeeping' figure.

The usual items on the Expenditure side of these Accounts are:—Housekeeping; Servants' wages; Rent and Taxes; Repairs; Furniture and Stationery; Candles; Horsekeeping; Travelling expenses; Letters; Bread and Wine (Sacrament); Poor; Buns (i.e. for the Lovefeast).

The Receipts from the Bands and Classes are given above for reference, the figures being, of course, included in the totals on the previous pages.

BIBLIOGRAPHY

CONTEMPORARY MSS.

Account of Cash receiv'd and disburs'd by the Society in London under ye direction of the Reverend Mr. John and Chas. Wesley—1766-1803.
(At the Methodist Book Room, London.)

Congregation of Protestant Dissenters of the Presbyterian Denomination, at Lewin's Mead, Bristol.
Records :—Minute Book, 1692-1774.
        Vestry Minute Book, 1793-1807.
        Annual Meetings Minute Book, 1774-1837.
        Poor Fund Cash Book, 1690-1738.
        Church Cash Book, 1690-1787.
(At the Unitarian Church, Lewin's Mead, Bristol.)

Memorandums, Remarks, and Occurences, Transacted in the Borough of Reading during the two Mayoralties of John Watts, Esqre., collected by him. c. 1722.
(At the Public Library, Reading.)

Papers relating to Methodism—1739-1759.
(At Dr. Williams's Library, London. Ref. Jones B 53, 11.)

Records of Nonconformity in the eighteenth century.
No. 4.—The Evans List.
    5.—Comparative statement of Nos. 4 and 6.
    6.—The Thompson List.
   18.—'A View of the Dissenting Interest in London of the Presbyterian and Independent Denominations from the year 1695 to the 25 December, 1731, with a postscript of the Present State of the Baptists.'
(At Dr. Williams's Library.)

The Records of the Congregational Church of Christ in Southampton —from 1688.
(At Above Bar Church, Southampton.)

CONTEMPORARY PRINTED SOURCES—including works written before, but published since, 1800

'A Layman.'	*The Right of Protestant Dissenters to a Complete Toleration.* 2nd edition, London, 1789.
Ames.	*De Conscientia.* Amsterdam, 1630.
Anon.	*A Brief Survey of the Legal Liberties of the Dissenters.* London, 1714.
do.	*The Life of Mr. Thomas Firmin.* London, 1698.
do.	*The New Whole Duty of Man.* 25th edition, 1780.
do.	*The Religious Assemblies of the People called Quakers vindicated.* 2nd edition, London, 1682/3.
do.	*The Remonstrance of the Suffering-People of God, called Quakers: Clearing their Innocency from the Many false Aspersions, Slanders, and Suggestions, which are lately come abroad in the Nation causelessly upon them.* London, 1665.
Barclay, Robert.	*An Apology for the . . . Quakers.* 9th edition (English), Dublin, 1800.

Baxter, Richard. *The Poor Husbandman's Advocate to Rich Racking Landlords.* Edit. by Powicke and reprinted from *The Bulletin of the John Rylands Library,Vol.* 10, *No.* 1, under the title *The Reverend Richard Baxter's Last Treatise.*

do. *The Practical Works of the Rev. Richard Baxter: with a life of the author, by the Rev. Wm. Orme,* London, 1830, in twenty-three vols. :—
    Vols. ii-vi.—The Christian Directory.
        xvii.—How to do Good to Many.
        xix.—The Poor Man's Family Book.

Bellers, John. *Proposals for Raising a College of Industry.* London, 1696.

do. *An Epistle to Friends, Concerning the Education of Children.* London, 1697.

do. *Essays about the Poor, Manufactures, Trade, Plantations, and Immorality.* London, 1699.

do. *To the Lords and other Commissioners, appointed by the Queen to take care of the Poor Palatines.* 1709.

do. *Some Reasons for an European State.* 1710.

do. *An Essay Towards the Improvement of Physick. In Twelve Proposals. With an Essay for Imploying the Able Poor.* 1714.

do. *An Epistle to the Quarterly Meeting of London and Middlesex.* 1718.

do. *An Essay for Imploying the Poor to Profit.* London, 1723.

do. *To the Yearly, Quarterly, and Monthly Meetings of Great Britain and Elsewhere.* 1723. (This Epistle was sent along with the previous work, which had been originally presented to Parliament.)

do. *An Epistle to Friends of the Yearly, Quarterly, and Monthly Meetings; concerning the Prisoners, and sick, in the prisons, and Hospitals of Great Britain.* 1724.

do. *To the Lords and Commons in Parliament assembled. A Supplement to the Proposal for a College of Industry.* N.D.

(Besse.) *A Brief Account of many of the Prosecutions of the People call'd Quakers.* London, 1736.

Brome. *The Snake in the Grass: or, Satan Transform'd into an Angel of Light.* 3rd edition. London, 1698.

Boswell. *Life of Samuel Johnson.* Edit. Fitzgerald, 1897.

Bunyan. *A Relation of the Imprisonment of Mr. John Bunyan . . . in* 1660.
Grace Abounding to the Chief of Sinners. Reprinted and edit. by Smellie, in one volume, London, 1897.

do. *Life and Death of Mr. Badman.* Edit. Dr. John Brown, C.U.P., 1905.

Burnet, Bp. *History of My Own Time. The Reign of Charles the Second.* Edit. Airy, 2 vols., Oxford, 1897.

Calamy. *Saints' Memorials: or, Words fitly spoken by Calamy and Others.* London, 1674.

Chamberlain, Peter. *A Scourge for a Den of Thieves.* London, 1659.

Coke & Moore. *The Life of the Rev. John Wesley, A.M.* London, 1822 (first published, 1792).

Defoe, Daniel. *A Tour through England and Wales.* 2 vols. Everyman.

do. *Giving Alms no Charity.* London, 1704.

do. *The Complete English Tradesman.* 2nd edit., London, 1727.

Defoe, Daniel. *The Earlier Life and the Chief Earlier Works of Daniel Defoe.* Edit. Henry Morley, London, 1889.

do. *Memoirs of the Life and Eminent Conduct of. . . Daniel Williams, D.D.* London, 1718.

do. ('Andrew Moreton') *Everybody's Business is Nobody's Business.* London, 3rd edition, 1725.

Eden. *The State of the Poor.* 3 vols., London, 1797.

F(irmin), T(homas). *Some Proposals for the employment of the Poor, and for the Prevention of idleness and consequence thereof Begging. . . .* London, 1681.

Flavell. *Husbandry Spiritualized.* 1674.

Fox, George. *The Journal of George Fox.* 2 vols., 1902, Bi-centenary edition, Society of Friends.

do. *The Vials of the Wrath of God. . . .* London, 1654.

F(ox), G(eorge). *A Warning to all the Merchants in London and such as buy and sell.* London, 1658.

Godwyn. *Phanatical Tenderness; or the claims of the Nonconformists exemplified in the practices of many of them in Bristol. . . .* London, 1684.

Gouge. *Riches Increased by giving to the Poor: or, Mr. Thomas Gouge's surest and safest way of thriving.* London, 1709.

Haines, Richard. *The Prevention of Poverty.* London, 1674.

do. *Proposals for Building in every County a Working-Almshouse or Hospital.* London, 1677.

do. *A Model of Government for the Good of the Poor.* London, 1678.

do. *Provision for the Poor.* London, 1678.

do. *England's Weal and Prosperity Proposed.* London, 1679 (?).

do. *A Breviat of some Proposals . . . for the speedy restoring of the Woollen Manufacture.* London, 1697.

do. *A Method of Government for such Publick Working Alms Houses.* London N.D.
(For Haines' pamphlets, see B.M. 1027, i. 16.)

Hale, Sir Matthew. *A Discourse Touching Provision for the Poor.* London, 1683.

do. *The Counsels of a Father in four letters . . . (and) the Good Steward at the Great Audit.* 4th edition, London, 1834.

do. *Contemplations Moral and Divine.* 1689.

Hankin. *Reflections on the Infamy of Smuggling. . .* London, 1790.

Howard. *The State of the Prisons in England and Wales.* 2nd edition, 1780.

Kiffin. *Life of Kiffin by himself.* Edit. Orme, London, 1823.

L(awson), T(homas). *An Appeal to the Parliament concerning the Poor, that there may not be a Beggar in England.* London, 1660 (B.M. 8275, a, 6).

(L'Estrange, Roger.) *Remarks on the Growth and Progress of Nonconformity.* London, 1682.

Locke. *Four Letters on Toleration.* London, 1870, reprint of 7th edition, 1758.

do. *Two Treatises of Civil Government.* Everyman.

Lord, J. H. *A Memorial of Squire Brooke, of Fieldhouse.* London, 2nd edition, 1783.

Macdonald, John. *Memoirs of an Eighteenth-century Footman.* Edit. Beresford. London, 1927.

McGlothlin. *Baptist Confessions of Faith.* London, 1910.

Mandeville.   *The Fable of the Bees: or, Private Vices, Public Benefits.* 2 vols., Oxford, 1924, edit. Kaye.

Mather,   *Twenty-three Sermons on Various Subjects.* London,
   Nathanael.   1701.

'Minutes.'   See end of this Section.

Morgan, James.   *The Life and Death of Mr. Thomas Walsh, composed in great part from the accounts left by himself.* London, 1762.

Myles, William.   *A Chronological History of the People called Methodists.* 3rd edition (enlarged), London, 1803.

Neal.   *History of the Puritans.* Toulmin's edition, vols. iv. and v. 1822.

Osborn.   *Works of Francis Osborn.* 7th edition, London, 1673.

Packington,   *The Gentleman's Calling.* London, 1662.
   Lady Dorothy.

do.   *The Ladies' Calling.* Oxford, 1693.

do. (?)   *The Whole Duty of Man.* 1703, also edited by Hawkins in 1842.

Pepys.   *The Diary of Samuel Pepys.* 9 vols., 1894, edit. Wheatley.

do.   *Private Correspondence and Miscellaneous Papers of Samuel Pepys,* 1679-1703. 2 vols., 1926, edit. Tanner.

Petty, Sir Wm.   *The Economic Writings of Sir Wm. Petty together with Observations upon the Bills of Mortality more probably by Capt. John Graunt.* 2 vols., C.U.P., 1899.

do.   *The Petty Papers: Some unpublished writings of Sir Wm. Petty from the Bowood Papers.* 2 vols., London, 1927.

Philo-Anglicus,   *Bread for the Poor. . . .* London, 1678 (B.M. 1027,
   Gent.   i. 16).

Price, Richard.   *A Discourse on the Love of our Country.* London, 1790.

do.   *Two Tracts on Civil Liberty.* London, 1778.

Priestley, J.   *An Essay on the First Principles of Government.* 2nd edition, London, 1771.

do.   *A View of the Principles and Conduct of the Protestant Dissenters, with respect to the Civil and Ecclesiastical Constitution of England.* 2nd edition, London, 1769.

'Reports.'   See end of this Section.

Society of   *Extracts from the Book of Christian Discipline of the*
   Friends.   *Religious Society of Friends in Great Britain.* London, 1884.

do.   *London Yearly Meeting During 250 Years.* London, 1919.

Steele, Richard.   *The Tradesman's Calling. . . .* London, 1684.

Told, Silas.   *An Account of the Life and Dealings of God with Silas Told . . . written by Himself.* Salford, 1806.

(Tracts.)   *Lord Somers' Collection of Tracts.* 2nd edition, London, 1814.

do.   *Stuart Tracts*: 1603-1693. Edit. Firth, 1903.

do.   *Later Stuart Tracts.* Intro. by Aitken, 1903.

Wade, John.   *Redemption of Time.* 1692.

Wesley, Charles.   *Journal.* 2 vols, 1849, edit. by Jackson.

Wesley, John.   *The Journal of the Rev. John Wesley.* 8 vols. London, 1909, edit. by Curnock.

do.   *The Letters of John Wesley.* Standard edition by Telford. 1931.

do.   *The Standard Sermons of John Wesley.* 2 vols. Annotated by Sugden. 1921.

Wesley, John.	*The Works of the Rev. John Wesley.* 14 vols. London, 1856, 11th edition by Jackson.
Wesley, John and Charles.	Hymns published by one or other, or both the Wesleys :—

1739, 'Hymns and Sacred Poems.' 138 hymns.
1744, 'Hymns for Times of Trouble.' 6 hymns.
?1744 (later edition, 1770), 'Hymns for the nativity of our Lord.' 18 hymns.
1745, 'Hymns for Times of Trouble and Persecution.' 2nd edition. 29 hymns.
?1746, 'Hymns for the Watch Night.' 11 hymns.
1749, 'Hymns and Sacred Poems,' by Charles Wesley. 2 vols., Bristol. 455 hymns.
1756, 'Hymns for the Year 1756, particularly for the Fast-day, Feby 6th.' Bristol. 17 hymns.
1758, 'Hymns of Intercession for All Mankind.' Bristol. 40 hymns.
?1761, 'Hymns for New Year's Day.' J.H. 7 hymns.
1765, 'Select Hymns designed chiefly for the Use of the People called Methodists,' with tunes. 2nd edition 'corrected and enlarged.' 149 hymns.
1767, 'Hymns for the Use of Families and on Various Occasions.' C.W. Bristol. 166 hymns.
1772, 'Preparations for Death, in several hymns.' London. J.W. 40 hymns.
1775, 'Hymns for Ascension Day.' J.W. London. 7 hymns.
1780, 'Hymns written in the Time of the Tumults, June, 1780.' Bristol. 13 hymns.
1780, 'A Collection of Hymns for the Use of the People called Methodists.' London. 525 hymns.
1782, 'Hymns for the National Fast, February 8, 1782.' London. 15 hymns.
1786, 'Hymns of Petition and Thanksgiving for the Promise of the Father.' London. 32 hymns.

Whitefield, G.	*Twenty-three Sermons on Various Subjects.* London, 1745. New edition.
do.	*The Works of the Rev. George Whitefield.* 8 vols. London, 1771.
Wilberforce.	*An Appeal . . . in behalf of the Negro Slaves in the West Indies.* London, 1823.
Winstanley, Jerrard.	*The Law of Freedom in a Platform: or, True Magistracy Restored.* London, 1652.
Woodforde, James.	*Diary of a Country Parson.* Edit. Beresford, O.U.P., 1926. 5 vols.
Woodward, Josiah.	*An Account of the Rise and Progress of the Religious Societies in the City of London.* 2nd edition (enlarged), London, 1698.
Young, Arthur.	*Six Months Tour through the North of England.* 2nd edition, 1771.

CONTEMPORARY PRINTED MINUTES AND RECORDS

(Baptist.)	Minutes of the General Assembly of the General Baptist Churches in England, with kindred records. Edit. Whitley. 2 vols. London (commences 1654).
do.	The Records of a Church of Christ, meeting in Broadmead, Bristol, 1640-1687. Edit. Underhill, for the Hanserd Knollys Society.

(Methodist.)   Minutes of the Methodist Conferences, from the First, held in London, by the late Rev. John Wesley, A.M., in the year 1744. Vol. 1, 1744-1798, London, 1812; vol. 2, 1799-1807, London, 1813.

do.   Another edition of the same, including other information, 1862.

(Nottingham-   Nottinghamshire County Records. Edit. Copnall.
shire.)   Nottingham, 1915.

CALENDARS : PERIODICAL PUBLICATIONS : WORKS OF REFERENCE

Baptist Historical Society, Transactions, 1908-1922.
Baptist Quarterly (incorporating the Baptist Historical Society's Transactions), from 1922.
Calendars of State Papers Domestic.
Congregational Historical Society : Transactions, from 1901.
Dictionary of National Biography.
Economica, June 1925 : Belasco, article on John Bellers.
Economic Journal Supplement, Economic History, vol. 1, pp. 275-279 : Belasco, article on The Labour Exchange Idea in the Seventeenth Century.
Extracts from State Papers relating to Friends, 1654-1672. London, 1913.
Friends' Historical Society, Journal, from 1903.
Historical MSS. Commission Reports.
Presbyterian Historical Society of England, Journal, from 1914.
Royal Commission on Licensing (England and Wales), 1929-31, Report, Appendix 2. Cmd. 3988.
The Annual Register, 1758-1800.
The Baptist Annual Register, 1790-1793; 1794-1797; 1798-1801. Edit., John Rippon.
The Gentleman's Magazine, 1731-1800.
The Harleian Miscellany. 12 vols., London, 1808 and 1810.
The Holborn Review, July, 1924. (George Fox Tercentenary.)
The Reading and Oxford Gazette, 1723-1800 (various numbers in this period—Reading Public Library).
Unitarian Historical Society, Transactions, from 1917.
Wesley Historical Society, Proceedings, from 1897.

SECONDARY AUTHORITIES AND OTHER WORKS

Anon.   *A Sketch of the History and Proceedings of the Deputies appointed to protect the Civil Rights of Protestant Dissenters.* London, 1814.
Arthur, William.   *The Successful Merchant: Sketches in the Life of Mr. S. Budgett.* London, 1852.
Ashton, T. S.   *Iron and Steel in the Industrial Revolution.* Manchester U.P., 1924.
Atmore.   *The Methodist Memorial.* Bristol, 1801.
Barclay.   *The Inner Life of the Religious Societies.* London, 1876.
Bate.   *The Declaration of Indulgence, 1672: A Study in the Rise of Organized Dissent.* Liverpool U.P., 1908.
Beer.   *A History of British Socialism.* Vol I, 1919.
Beresford.   *Gossip of the Seventeenth and Eighteenth Centuries.* London, 1924.
Bland, Brown, and Tawney.   *English Economic History Select Documents,* Part 3. London, 1925.
Blanshard.   *The Life of Samuel Bradburn, The Methodist Demosthenes.* London, 1871.